WARRINGTON AT WORK

JANICE HAYES

AMBERLEY

First published 2017

Amberley Publishing
The Hill, Stroud
Gloucestershire, GL5 4EP

www.amberley-books.com

Copyright © Janice Hayes & Culture Warrington, 2017

The right of Janice Hayes to be identified as the Author
of this work has been asserted in accordance with the
Copyrights, Designs and Patents Act 1988.

ISBN 978 1 4456 6995 3 (print)
ISBN 978 1 4456 6996 0 (ebook)

British Library Cataloguing in Publication Data.
A catalogue record for this book is available
from the British Library.

Origination by Amberley Publishing.
Printed in the UK.

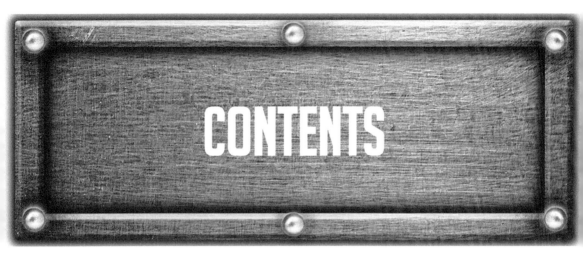

CONTENTS

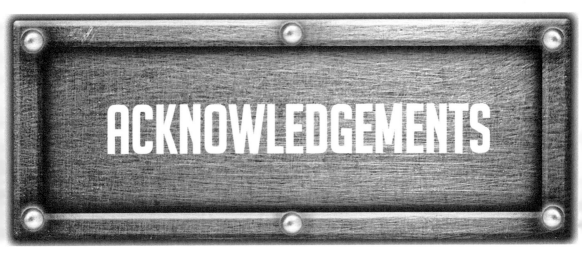

ACKNOWLEDGEMENTS

This book has been compiled from the records held by Culture Warrington's Archives section and the majority of images are from the collections held by Warrington Museum on behalf of the town. Other images appear courtesy of the *Warrington Guardian* and Warrington & Co. Thanks are due to all those who have documented Warrington at work and every effort has been made to trace the copyright holders.

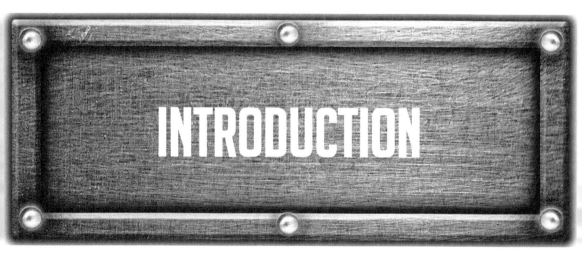

INTRODUCTION

By the late eighteenth century Warrington was an established market town at the hub of the national transport network. Industry was just appearing at Bank Quay while the intellectual excellence of Warrington Academy led some to describe the town as 'The Athens of the North'.

Early twenty-first-century Warrington has embarked on a major regeneration of its retail offer. Its businesses have links to the national and international road network and connectivity with national rail and regional waterways and airports. The massive soap and chemicals works dominate Bank Quay and for many Warringtonians is the only visible sign of industry in the town. The emerging city has a new university campus and is investing in the development of its future workforce. In 2017 Warrington was included in the *Sunday Times*' '101 Best Places to Live' and has ambitions to be a future UK Capital of Culture.

Despite these striking parallels Warrington has undergone significant changes in its economy in the intervening centuries, and the lives of its workers have changed almost beyond recognition. Many of these changes were the result of national and international developments while others were locally driven. From the late eighteenth century until the mid-twentieth century significant industrial and economic growth came through the efforts of local entrepreneurs and investors. Local families such as Patten, Stubs, Parr, Lyon, Greenall, Walker, Crosfield, Rylands, Greenings, Locker and Monk established locally based businesses and many became closely involved with local politics. By the twenty-first century the majority of Warrington's businesses are national or international companies with minimal involvement in the daily life of the town.

For much of the twentieth century Warrington was known as 'The Town of Many Industries', and the smells and sounds of everyday working life were clearly evident even in the town centre. The *Warrington Examiner* described a typical scene at Bishop's Wharf near Bridge Foot in 1933:

> Here the explorer would smell strange smells. The curious odour of molten iron, the smell of hot rubber, the sharp tang of hides in pickle, the rich, dry smell of grain. He will hear the merry rattle of chains and the thud of grain sacks, the impatient throb of laden motor-lorries and the laboured tread of patient dray horses. Tied up to the wharf itself are business like stout little river boats into whose capacious holds donkey engines drop load upon load of Warrington wire that shines like new silver, and bags of nails, making the lumbering, honest-looking craft strain against their ropes.

Less attractive was the pall of industrial smog that hung over much of the town until the mid-1960s but many accepted this as the price of employment. Workers' houses were often crammed close to the noise and smells of the workplace. Factories, foundries and tanneries were badly lit, unventilated and full of dangerous machinery and hazardous chemicals. Working hours were not controlled by laws and paid holidays not guaranteed. Sickness benefits and pensions were not introduced until the early twentieth century and equal pay was unheard of until the 1970s and beyond.

The business parks and distribution warehouses of twenty-first-century Warrington are home to workers who could expect to spend their day in well-lit, safe environments and enjoy paid annual leave and bank holidays. However, the concept of a job for life has disappeared and the factory floor has given way to working in banks and call centres, coffee bars and pizza parlours, or as warehouse pickers serving the online shopping boom.

Twenty-first-century Warrington has a vision for its future through Warrington & Co., the organisation tasked with realising Warrington Borough Council's ambitions for economic success. As 'Warrington Means Business'– the new master plan for the centre and new development quarters – was launched in 2017 uncertainties about the outcome of Brexit for a local economy with close European links loomed on the horizon. Even the future of the mooted Northern Powerhouse and investment in the much-vaunted HS2 rail stood in the balance.

However, whatever the outcome nationally, Warrington can call on its long heritage of economic resilience to shape its future success.

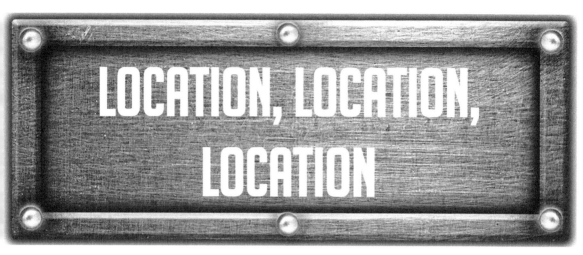

LOCATION, LOCATION, LOCATION

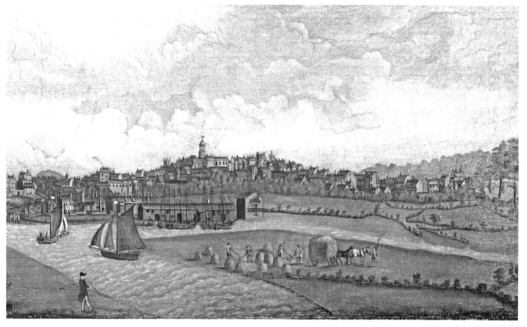

Donbavand's view of Warrington in 1772 shows the bridge (far right), the town centre, and flat-bottom barges sailing up river past Bank Hall (far left.).

Location was the key to Warrington's successful emergence as a centre of industry. Warrington Bridge had been vital to the regional and national road network since the thirteenth century. During the eighteenth century major improvements to water communications enhanced Warrington's importance. In the late 1690s the Mersey was deepened and made navigable from Runcorn to Bank Quay by the Patten family. In the 1720s the Mersey-Irwell Navigation Co. made the river navigable for flat-bottomed barges and small barges, linking Liverpool to Manchester via Warrington. 'Warrington may in some measure be considered as a port town', wrote Aikin in 1795. Baines Directory of 1825 recorded that, 'The communication between Manchester and Liverpool, by means of this navigation is incessant, and the brick dust coloured sails of the barges are seen every hour of the day on their passage, flickering on the wind.'

Despite increased river traffic Warrington's sail cloth manufacturing industry was in decline by the early nineteenth century. When Arthur Young visited Warrington in 1769 he found that the industry employed around '300 weavers and … they reckon twenty spinners and two or three hands to every weaver'.

Demand for sailcloth was strongest in wartime and possibly half the cloth for Nelson's naval battles against France's Napoleonic Empire was woven in the town. At the peace of 1815 demand for sailcloth fell into terminal decline. Some workers found employment in other branches of the textile industry while at least one major manufacturer (Rylands) diversified into the wire industry.

A MARKET TOWN

Warrington's bridge made it a regional and national transport node standing on the main road between London, Carlisle and Scotland. London-bound stagecoaches from Liverpool passed through the town twice daily on six days a week. Other coaches linked Warrington with Wigan and Kendal, Manchester to Liverpool and Chester to York. By the 1820s between sixty and seventy coaches passed through the town daily carrying small freight as well as passengers and the town centre inns flourished. Wagons and packhorses carrying heavier goods were also routed through the town.

By the 1840s Warrington's Market Place had become a focus for country people trading grain, vegetables and meat at the weekly markets and also livestock at the fortnightly Wednesday fairs. Dairy produce such as farm fresh butter and cheese was also on offer at the temporary trestle tables in front of the Barley Mow Inn.

Warrington also had a thriving fishing industry. The Universal Directory of 1792 recorded that, 'In the river are caught sturgeons, greenbacks, mullets, sand eels, lobsters, shrimps, prawns, and the best and largest cockles in all of England.' Overfishing and the growth of industry along the river banks had killed off the trade within another fifty years.

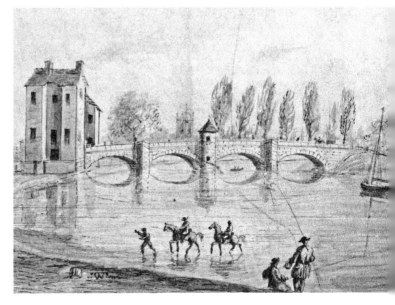

'There is no other bridge over the Mersey between Warrington and the sea, and none for miles upwards between it and Manchester.' (John Aiken describing Warrington Bridge in 1795.)

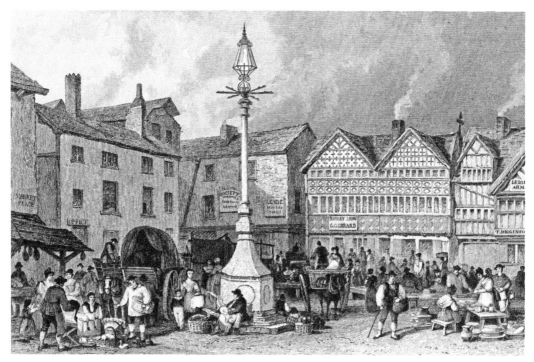

Warrington's bustling Market Place is seen here in the 1840s when it was a focal point for country traders from a wide radius.

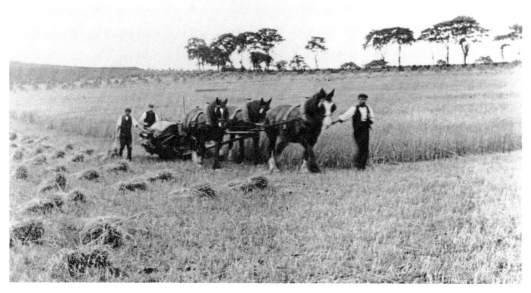

Even by the early twentieth century haymaking at Quarry Lane, Appleton, still followed the traditional farming calendar.

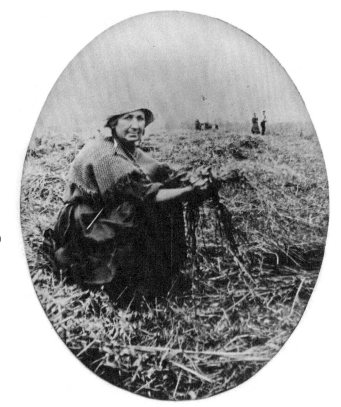

Right: Local farmers relied on seasonal itinerant labourers like this gleaner at Arpley to help with the harvests.

Below: Risley's mosslands produced abundant crops enabling local farmers to supply nearby markets such as Warrington with crops of cabbages, leeks, celery and potatoes.

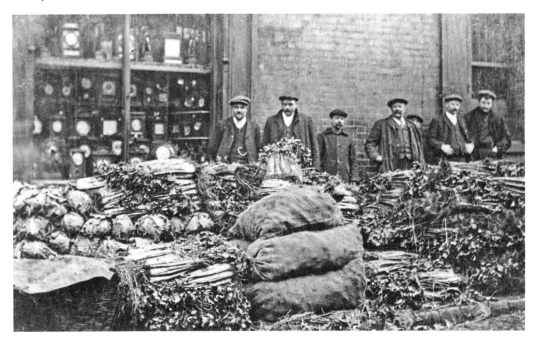

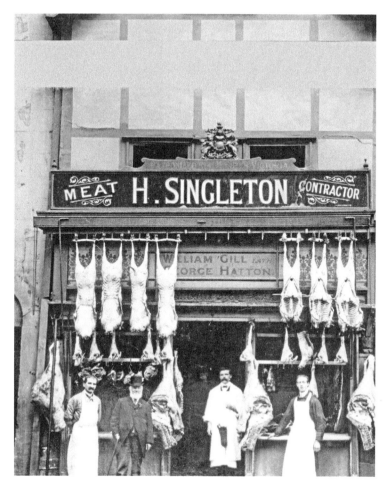

Left: Singleton & Stephenson's premises in Bridge Street, pictured in the late 1890s, was said to be the oldest established butcher's shop in England.

Below: Fishing for sparlings on the River Mersey in the 1790s, seen here from Knutsford Road.

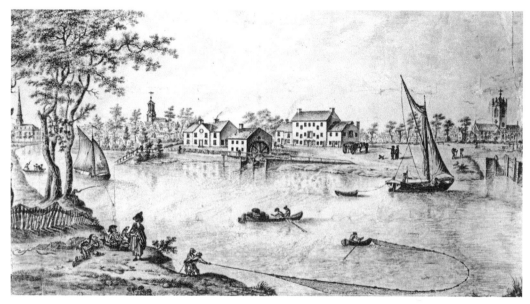

THE TOOLS TO DEVELOP INDUSTRY

By the end of the eighteenth century Warrington's developing port had been linked with the canal network meaning river traffic was no longer dependent on the tide. The canals opened up access to the Cheshire salt fields and linked Warrington to the nearby collieries. By the beginning of the nineteenth century Warrington had a waterway network for freight traffic linked to the ports of Liverpool, Hull and Bristol, as well as Manchester and the Pottery towns in the Midlands.

Besides access to vital raw materials, Warrington's industrial development was fostered by the entrepreneurial spirit of Peter Stubs and the innovative curriculum of Warrington Academy. As the landlord of the White Bear Inn in Bridge Street in the late 1770s, Stubs used the byproducts of his brewing activities in the hardening of files, making them superior to his competitors. At first he used outworkers from the surrounding area but later pioneered the factory age by centralising his workforce at Cockhedge, making Warrington a centre of tool production. More importantly he found new markets in the mechanics of the factory age by diversifying from files into a wide range of other tools needed to keep machinery running smoothly.

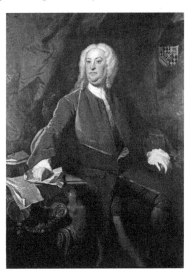

Right: Hamlet Winstanley's portrait shows wealthy businessman Thomas Patten, who commissioned famous architect James Gibbs to build his new mansion of Bank Hall (now Warrington's Town Hall).

Below: By 1772 Bank Quay was an industrial centre with warehouses, a glassworks (left) and Patten's copper-smelting works (seen above the sails of the central two boats).

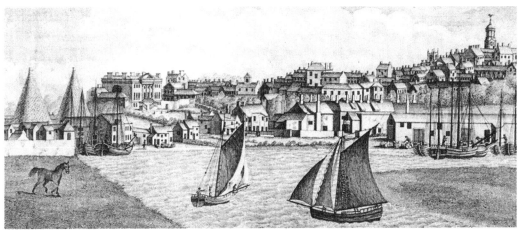

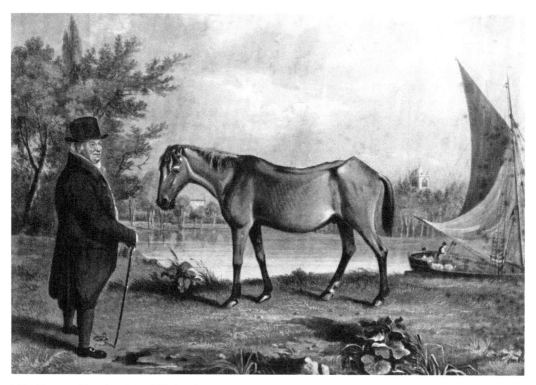

Workhorses like Old Billy (1760–1822) were a familiar sight towing barges on the local canal network. He was a popular character until his retirement to Latchford.

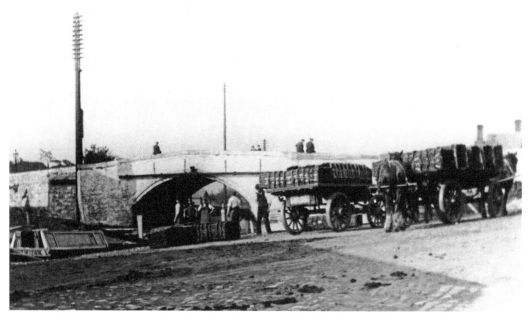

This busy scene at London Bridge, Stockton Heath, in 1908 shows goods being unloaded from the barges for onward travel by horse and cart.

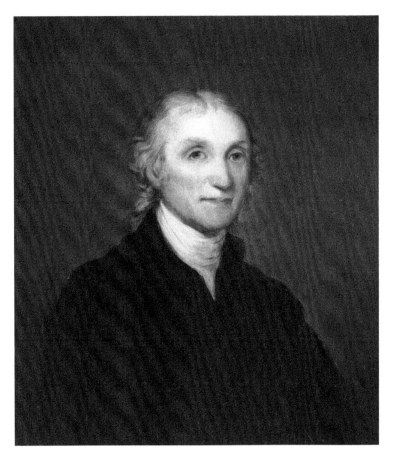

Right: Joseph Priestley, probably the greatest eighteenth-century scientist, came to Warrington Academy as a tutor in 1762.

Below: Warrington Academy opened in 1757 to provide a university education to those whose Nonconformist beliefs meant they could not gain entry to Oxford or Cambridge.

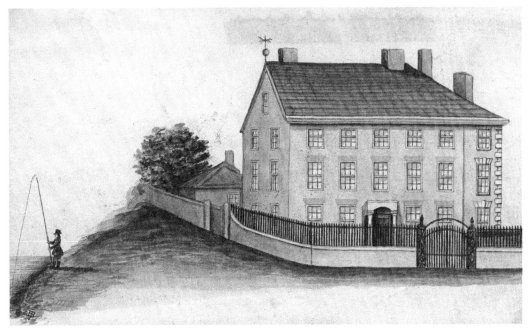

15

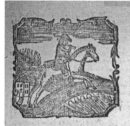 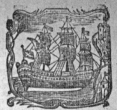

EYRES's WEEKLY JOURNAL, OR, THE WARRINGTON Advertiser

NUMB. 13.

From TUESDAY JUNE 8, to TUESDAY JUNE 15, 1756.

THURSDAY's POST.

From the EVENING POSTS, &c. *June 8.*

Since our last arrived a mail from Holland.

Petersburgh, (in Russia) May 11.

HE military and naval preparations in this empire go on with vigour: we have a squadron of twenty five men of war and frigates, which will be ready to put to sea in a few days; in order to escort between sixty and seventy gallies which are to proceed to the coast of Courland, there to take on board 30,000

The diet hath made an order that no person, who hath not a fixed residence and a certain number of acres of land, shall be elected a member of the house of peasants.

Marseilles, (in France) May 18. It is reported that twenty five battalions are to be sent to Minorca. We know with certainty that Marshal Richelieu has threatened the natives with death, who give any intelligence or succours whatever to the English.

PLANTATION NEWS.

Extract of a letter from St. Eustatia, Jan. 26.

'Yesterday a sloop arrived from the Cape, who brings advice, that two men of war, with some transports, sailed for the Mississippi, with a regiment of Swiss and other troops, and a great quantity of

Indians had attacked lieutenant Bull, and 30 men that were posted at the upper-end of the Great Carrying-place; that he, and some of his people were killed, and a small store, with some provisions in it, burnt; and that they were in pain for some of their battoes, which they feared were cut off by the enemy.

By the same express we are told, that sir William Johnson was again set out, with as many of the militia and Indians as his time would permit him to get together, and was determined to scour the woods on both sides of the Mohawks river, and proceed as far as Oswego, if he found it necessary.

Philadelphia, April 8. Cap. Rees, from Jamaica, informs us, that on his passage he spoke with the Weazel sloop of war, and that she had in company with her a large French schooner, which she took off of Leogane, bound in there from Martinico, laden with cocoa.

Williamsburg. April 16. By a letter from Win-

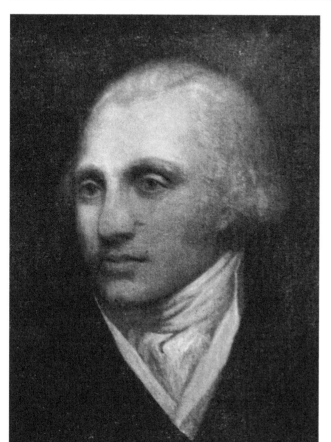

Above: William Eyres' Horsemarket Street press published the work of many of the Warrington Academy's distinguished tutors and initiated Lancashire's second oldest newspaper called *The Eyre's Weekly Journal* or *The Warrington Advertiser.*

Left: Peter Stubs was a Warrington entrepreneur who successfully developed his toolmaking business to meet the demands of the Industrial Revolution.

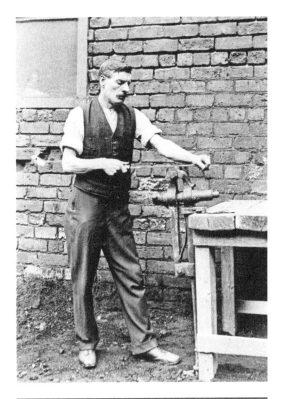

File-makers were among the worst paid workers in the town, despite their skills. After a seven-year apprenticeship wages were often less than those of unskilled labourers.

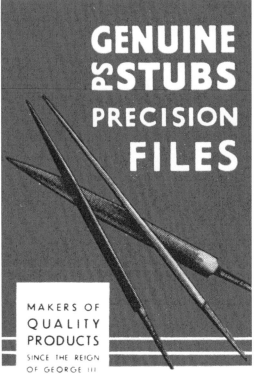

GENUINE PS STUBS PRECISION FILES

MAKERS OF QUALITY PRODUCTS SINCE THE REIGN OF GEORGE III

Leading engineer James Nasmyth regarded Stubs files as 'vastly superior to other files, both in the superiority of steel and in the perfection of the cutting'.

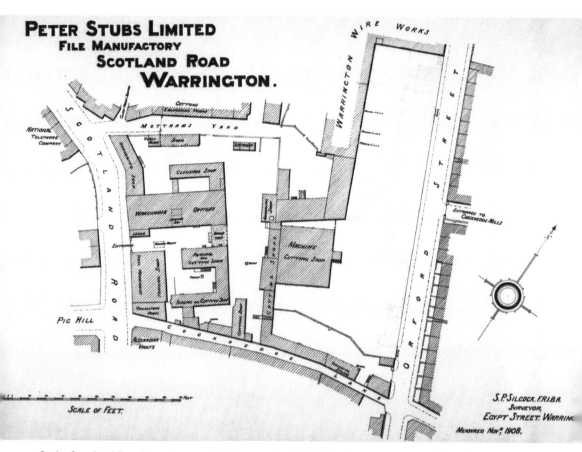

Stubs Scotland Road works were highly organised with forging, cutting, annealing, cleaning and hardening shops, warehouses and offices.

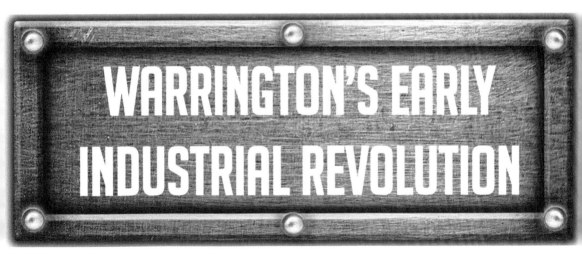

WARRINGTON'S EARLY INDUSTRIAL REVOLUTION

During the classical Industrial Revolution of 1750–1830 Warrington had all the ingredients necessary for economic expansion: cheap coal, proximity to Cheshire salt fields and easy access to ports and other manufacturing and commercial centres. However, the town had no direct link to the Manchester–Liverpool railway in 1831 and for a time it seemed as if it's development had stalled while its larger neighbours prospered. However, within fifty years Warrington factories would benefit from the completion of local links to the national railway networks.

Unlike neighbouring towns Warrington did not become a specialist in chemical production or draw on its tradition of linen and sailcloth manufacture to become a major cotton town. Instead Warrington developed as a town of many industries with two major industrial centres at Cockhedge and Bank Quay.

By the early nineteenth century Cockhedge was fast becoming Warrington's second major industrial site with Stub's tool factory joined by a cotton mill and glassworks. Meanwhile

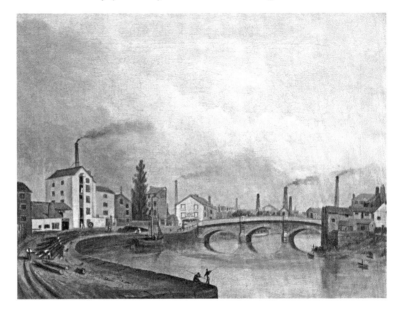

A view of Bridge Foot in the late 1830s with the new workplace chimneys of Howley visible behind the new Victoria Bridge.

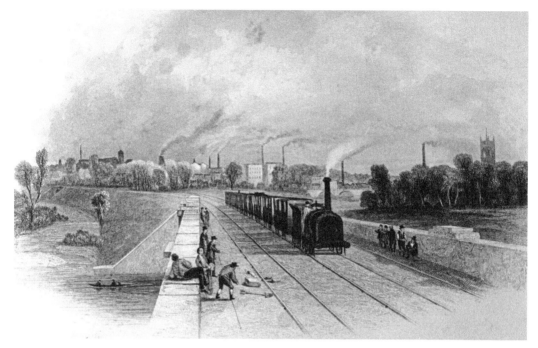

A locomotive leaves behind the belching factory chimneys of a newly industrialised Warrington as it leaves Bank Quay station in the late 1830s on the Grand Junction line.

a former local grocer, Joseph Crosfield, began the production of soap in a disused factory near Liverpool Road at Bank Quay in 1815 and by the 1860s Crosfield's had become one of the top five soap producers in the country.

By the 1840s Warrington was already engaged in fustian (or velvet) cutting and even when the cotton industry was at its peak in the 1920s only around 6 per cent of the town's workforce was employed in the industry but almost 20 per cent of the town's women workers worked in its mill.

PINS, FUSTIAN & COTTON

Pin-making was well established as Warrington's wire industry grew but initially some of the processes were done in the worker's home. Gradually small workshops developed in places like 'Pinner's Brow' off Orford Lane until Edelsten's established larger works to centralise the processes. Pin-making was usually done by young children who could often work a ten-hour day. The repetitive tasks often damaged their eyesight or deformed their developing muscles.

In the nineteenth century Fustian cutting took place in around forty small workshops scattered around the town. In 1912 William Netherwood introduced machinery into the United Velvet Cutter's new factory in Hale Street. Business expanded to become the largest in Britain and possibly Europe but still only employed around 450 people by 1930 when it was at its peak.

In 1787 Peel's cotton mill at Latchford was one of the earliest mills in the north-west to be powered by steam. At its peak in the 1820s the town had over twenty firms engaged in cotton spinning or weaving. The smaller mills could not survive the cotton crisis caused by the American Civil War of the 1860s and only Armitage & Rigby's Cockhedge Mill remained.

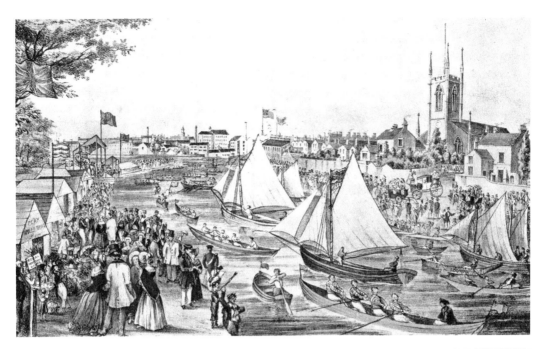

Above: The factories in the distance are already polluting the river as Warrington's annual regatta sails towards the town centre in the early 1840s, passing St James's Church on Wilderspool Causeway.

Right: John Edelsten owned a number of pin works employing over 400 workers including the Mersey Pin Works on Knutsford Road (seen here).

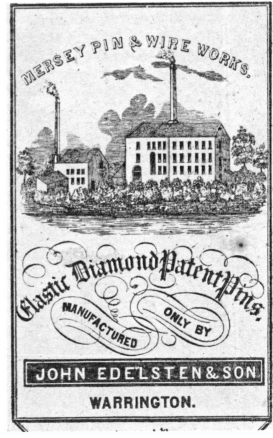

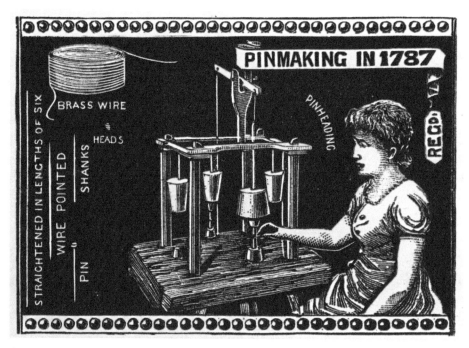

A young girl uses the stamping block in the monotonous task of pin-heading. Several hundred children were employed in pin-making as their small fingers were more nimble than adults.

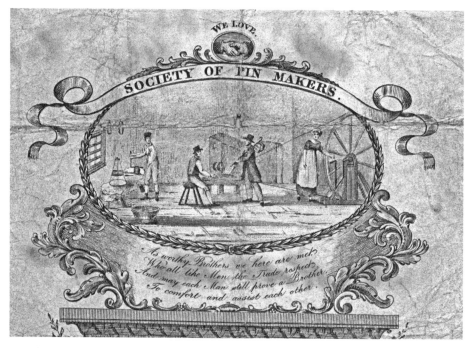

This Society of Pin-Makers' card of the 1840s shows the domestic scale of the industry and represents an early workers' organisation.

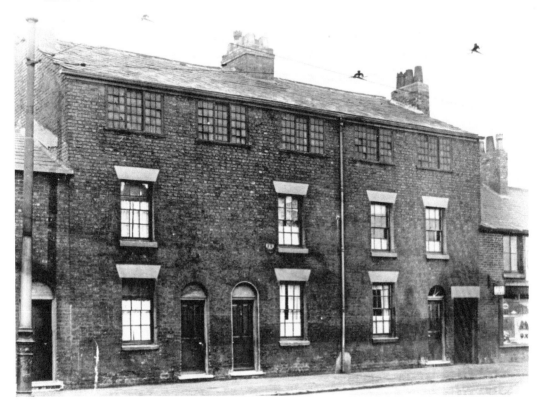

Right: Pin-makers used a wide variety of designs for their paper packaging to appeal to changing fashions.

Below: The fustian cutting workshop in Church Street with the workers' houses below and the long workshop running the length of the attics of the terrace.

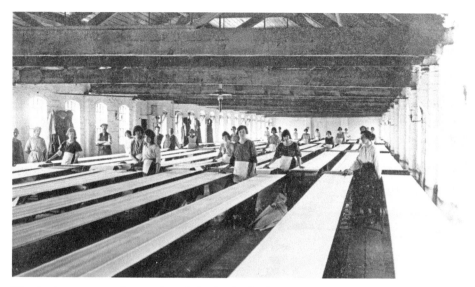

The fustian cutters who produced the finished velvet cloth worked along the line of the cloth stretched flat on a long table, often walking 150 miles a week.

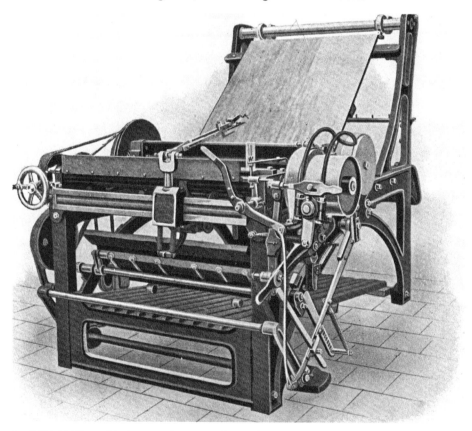

In 1911 William Netherwood invented a velvet-cutting machine, which was soon introduced into Warrington's works to speed up production.

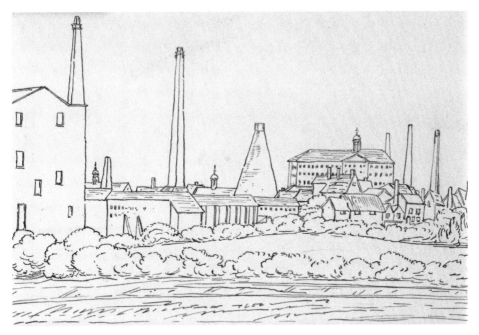

By the 1830s workers were relocating from the surrounding villages to Cockhedge to work at the crown glassworks and new cotton factory (right).

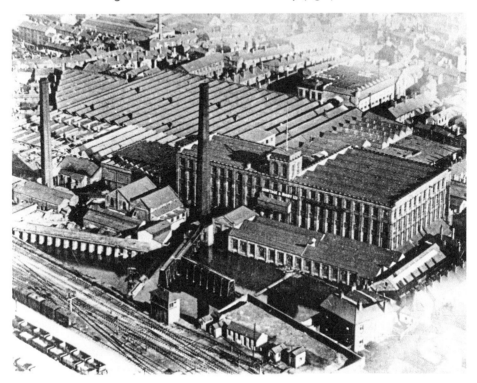

By the late 1890s terraced housing was crammed around Armitage & Rigby's cotton mill, which dominated Cockhedge and nearby Central Station.

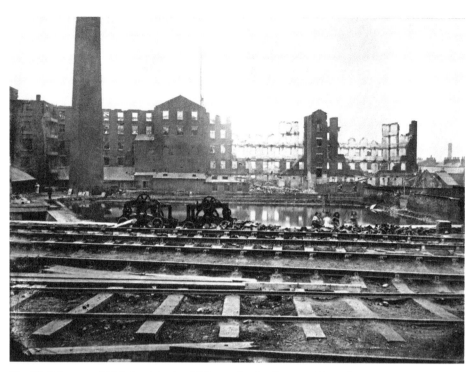

On 20 February 1896 Cockhedge Mill was badly damaged by a fire, which needed the attention of seventeen firemen and both the town's steam fire engines.

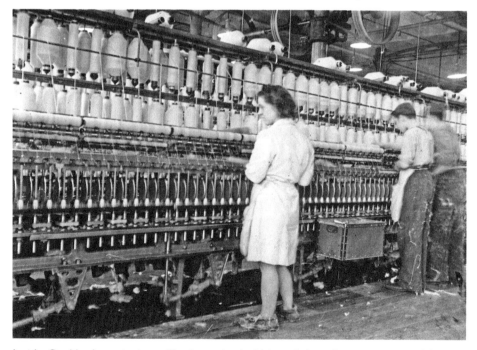

Inside Cockhedge spinning mill where the bobbins of threads were prepared for the weavers.

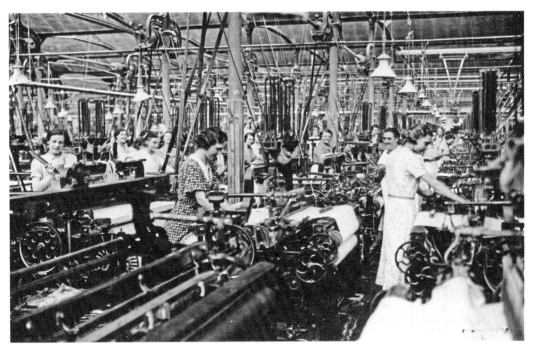

The clatter of looms at work in the weaving sheds was deafening and the women needed to lip-read if they wanted to chat.

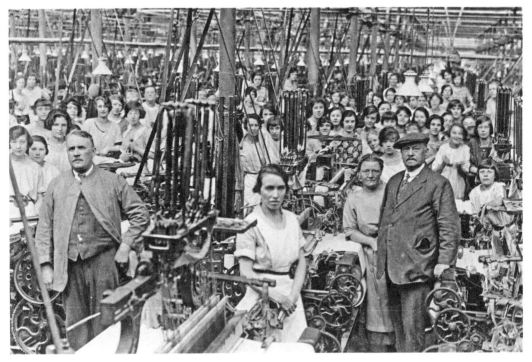

The majority of the weavers were women, with men mostly employed as mechanics and foremen. Weaving was well paid but women were expected to leave when they married.

GLASS, SOAP AND CHEMICALS

Warrington's glass industry was established at Bank Quay by Peter Seaman in 1757 and later operated by Perrin & Geddes & Co. In the late 1860s Robinson's established a separate operation nearby, called the Mersey Glassworks. Robinson's also had an interest in glassworks at Cockhedge and Orford Lane but it was the Mersey works that established their reputation for producing fine-cut glass tableware, which was shipped worldwide. The works covered 3 acres of land and employed around 180 workers. Cheaper foreign glass imports and inferior press-moulded glass helped to end Warrington's glass industry in the early twentieth century.

While glassmaking declined Crosfield's soap and chemicals operation prospered and the firm expanded south of the river, swallowing up former Cheshire farm land for its storage tanks. By 1884 there were soap wars at Bank Quay with the arrival of William Hesketh Lever and his 'Sunlight' soap. By 1887 Lever had to introduce additional soap pans as production increased twentyfold and his chemical site needed expansion. Lever was forced to relocate to Port Sunlight but in the early 1920s his old business rival Sir Arthur Crosfield, tired of manufacturing and sold the Bank Quay works to Lever Brothers.

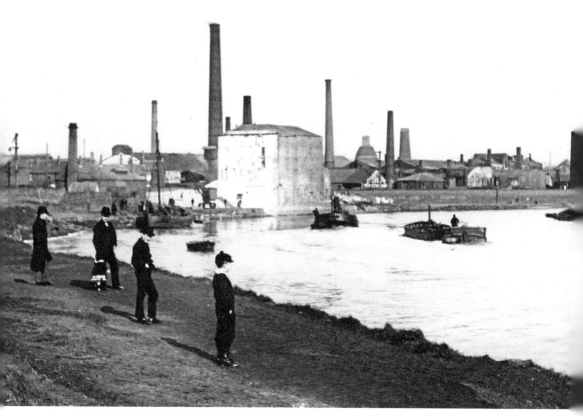

This 1890s view of Bank Quay shows Crosfield's soap works (right), the single cone of Robinson's glassworks in the background and Fairclough's Bank Quay Mill (centre).

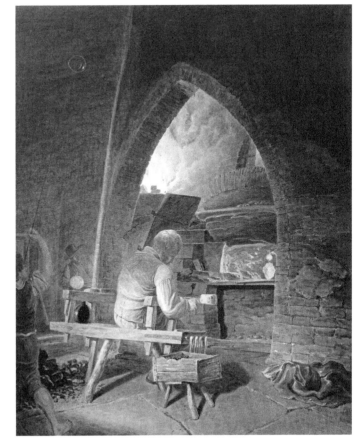

Right: A rare portrait of a skilled local glass-blower at work at Bank Quay in his 'chair' shaping the molten glass with the tools that are set out around him.

Below: A view inside Robinson's cutting shop in the late nineteenth century showing the large scale of their operations.

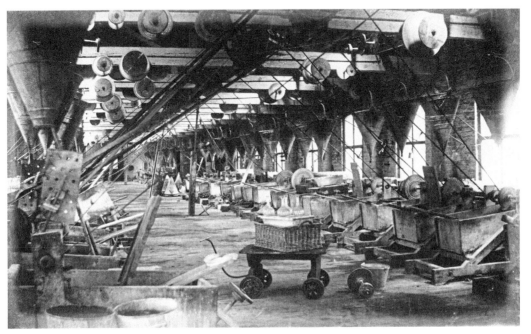

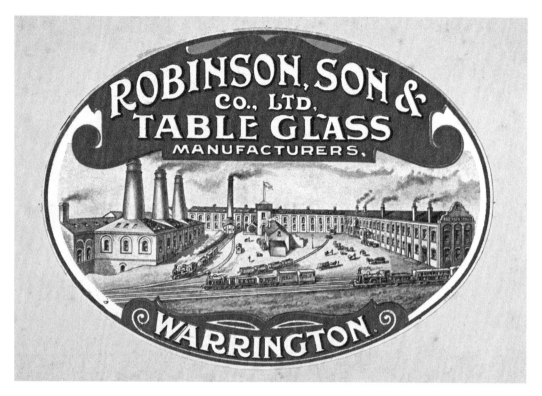

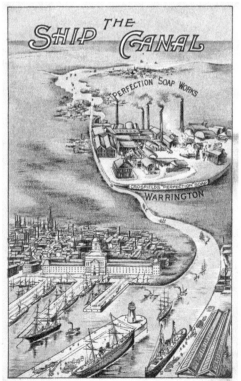

Above: Robinson's works had private railway sidings linking it to the main Bank Quay line.

Left: This early twentieth-century advertisement shows Crosfield's links to the port of Liverpool and Manchester Docks via the Manchester Ship Canal.

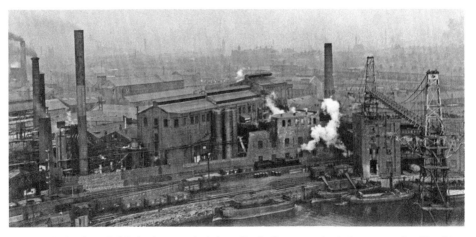

By the 1900s Crosfield's had expanded their Bank Quay works, linking it to the Cheshire side of the river by an early transporter bridge (right).

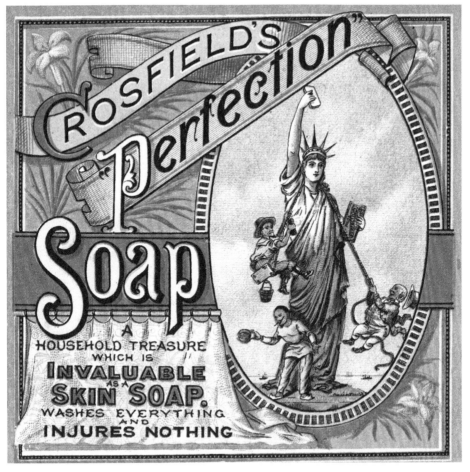

'Perfection' soap was one of Crosfield's bestselling brands, and this advert implies that it is popular all over the world.

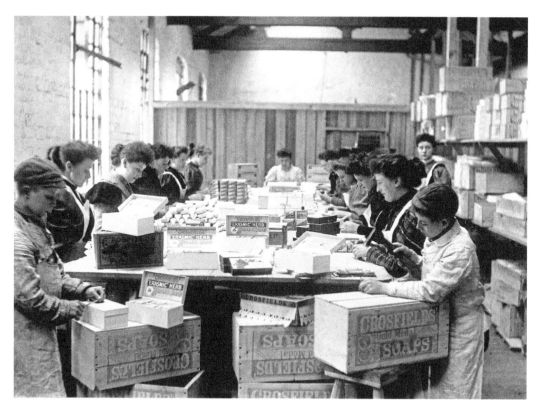

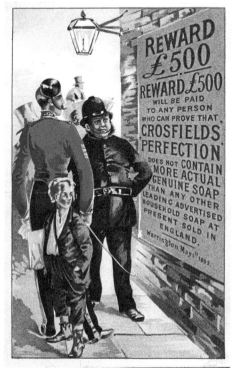

Above: Crosfield's 'Gold Medal' soaps are packed for despatch, including their trademark 'Erasmic Herb' toilet soap.

Left: Crosfield's were quick to adopt new marketing techniques and advances in colour printing in their advertising campaigns.

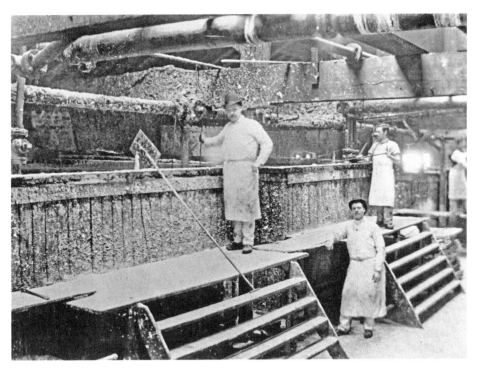

Soap production at Bank Quay expanded rapidly in the 1880s, but these soap pans belonged to their rival, William Hesketh Lever.

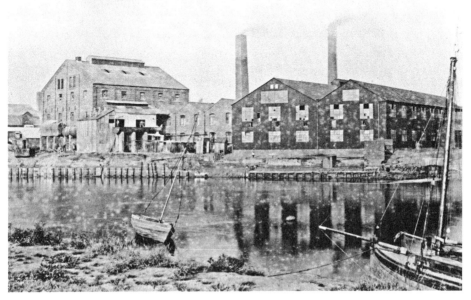

Lever's attempts to expand his Bank Quay works (seen here) were thwarted and he relocated his operations to Port Sunlight.

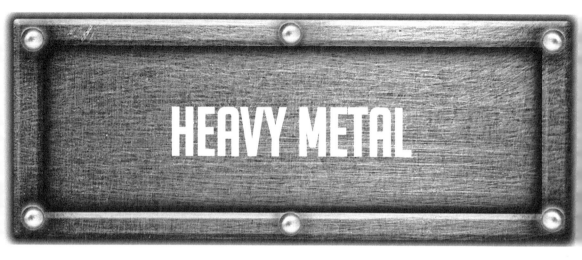

HEAVY METAL

Warrington's excellent transport network allowed industrialists to import all the necessary raw materials to develop a flourishing wire, iron and steel industry, which had become the town's major employer by the late nineteenth century.

Warrington was never a one-industry town but wire working was its most important trade. Wire making had first arrived in the eighteenth century with the firms of Houghton's and Greening's and by 1830 Ryland's wire works dominated, later followed by Locker's, Whitecross and the Firth Co.

The town's wire workers supplied the demands of other industries, producing woven wire ropes for collieries and shipping, gauze, perforated screens, sieves and conveyor belts, together with wire fencing and nails for builders.

The coming of the railways during the nineteenth century brought ironworks, which were concentrated in the Bank Quay and Dallam Lane areas, including Monks Hall & Co. and Pearson & Knowles. Warrington's iron works were indeed places of heavy industry, needing

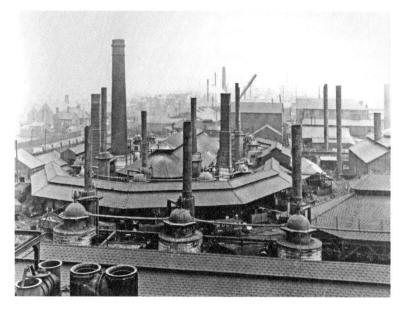

This early industrial photograph by Thomas Birtles shows the scale of Monks Hall & Co.'s ironworks by the end of the nineteenth century.

men of steel to endure the working conditions. Here was machinery on a gigantic scale: huge metal sheets and girders suspended from overhead cranes, roaring furnaces, intense heat and noise, flying sparks, and white-hot metal shooting past unwary workers.

Warrington's iron foundries were also at the heart of a domestic revolution that exploited gas as the new fuel for cooking and other household tasks. By 1900 Warrington's metal works were producing everything from gas cookers and fires to fine piano wire, sturdy wire ropes, steel girders, railway engine parts and bedsteads.

COME ON THE WIRE!

The 'Wire', the original nickname of the town's rugby league club, came from the term 'wire-pullers' or 'wire-drawers' who were the skilled craftsmen of the industry and earned at least three times as much as the labourers. Wire drawers had their own trade union that the galvanisers and other essential wire workers were not allowed to join.

While most wire works specialised in wire drawing, Locker specialised in woven wire that had a very wide variety of industrial and commercial uses. Wire mesh was needed for sieves and riddles in commercial processes such as flour milling, sand and gravels grading, and the production of cement, all fast-growing industries during the second half of the nineteenth century. Wire weaving would be the only section of the industry to adapt to the changing market conditions by the twenty-first century.

The Rylands and Greenings who owned Warrington's major wire works also played a prominent part in local life and politics. Frederick Monks not only served on the town council but left the greatest legacy of the town's connection with the iron industry when he presented the Town Hall Gates to Warrington on the 1895 Walking Day.

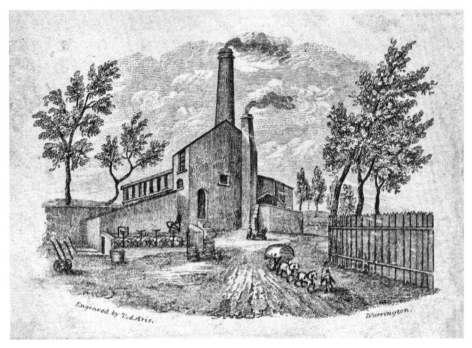

Ryland's early Church Street wire works, opened in 1817, grew to become one of the Warrington's busiest industrial sites by the late 1830s.

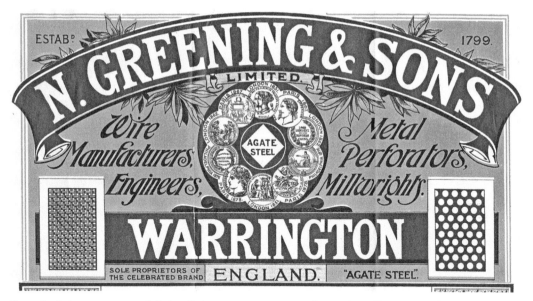

Greening's became one of Ryland's largest competitors from their Britannia Wire Works which opened at Bewsey in 1843.

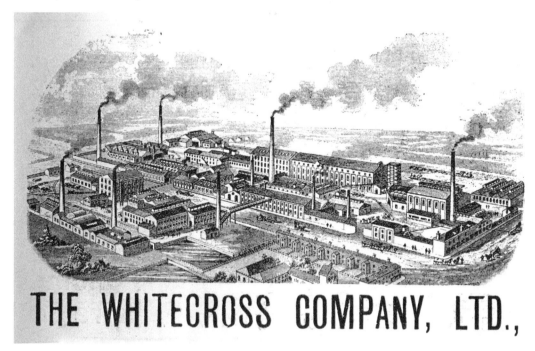

By this 1908 advertisement the Whitecross Wire Works was a major employer and dominated the town's skyline near the Town Hall.

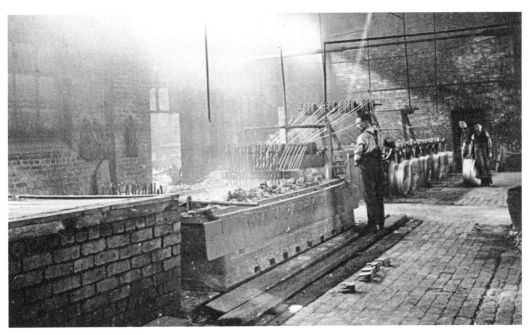

Wire works' labourers spent long hours breathing hazardous chemicals without protective clothing. Conditions in the galvanising plant where wire was coated with zinc to prevent corrosion were among the worst.

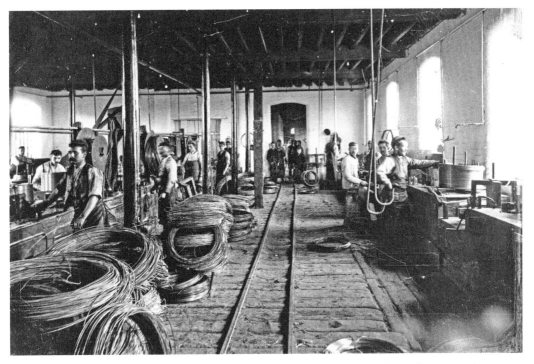

This interior shot of the Longford Wire, Iron and Steel Works in the early twentieth century shows the wire drawers hard at work on their benches.

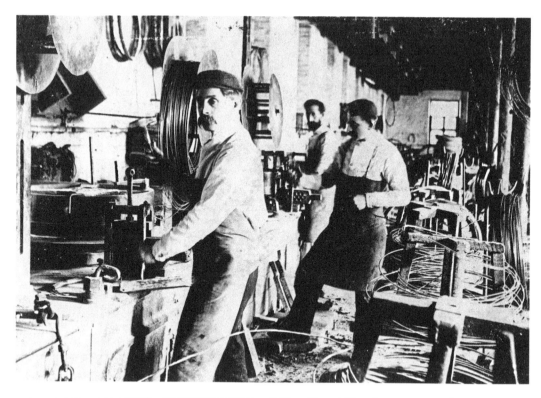

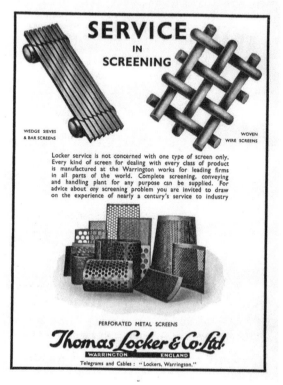

Above: Wire drawers were the aristocrats of the industry, earning higher wages than the unskilled workers and even drinking in separate rooms in their local pub.

Left: Thomas Locker & Co. was another major Warrington wire firm, specialising in wire weaving rather than wire drawing.

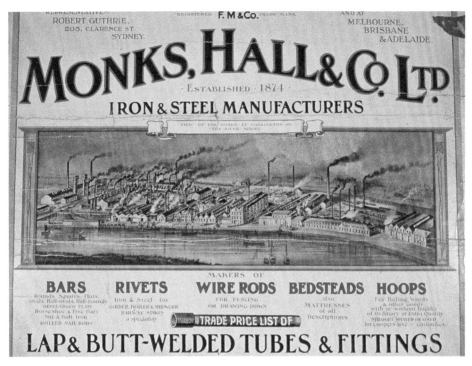

Monks, Hall & Co. became one of the world's largest producers of finished iron and steel, with forge mills, puddling furnaces, a tube works and a riveting plant.

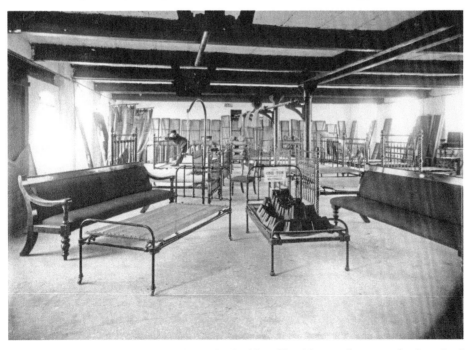

A newly made wire mattress withstands the 'One Ton Mattress' test at the Longford Wire, Iron & Steel Works.

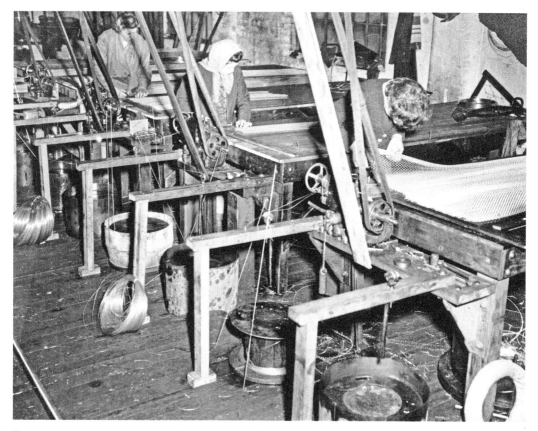

Spring mattress bases were produced at works like Monks Hall (seen here) until the mid-1960s when spring interior bases came into fashion.

FOUNDING A BRAVE NEW WORLD

Richmond's New World gas cookers were many twentieth-century housewives' preferred brand and their Latchford works was on a grand scale:

> The foundry is one of the largest of its kind in the North of England, with a daily output of between 40 to 50 tons of castings. The Enamelling Department is also the largest and the finest of its kind ... A highly-trained staff, using entirely new plant and extensive methods of production are constantly employed upon the manufacture of 'New World' cookers in 'Rado' enamelled finish. The grinding shops, the sand-blasting shops, machine shops, assembling shops, tin smiths' shops; water heating department, the department devoted to the manufacture of hotel cooking equipment; the Gas fire Radiant-making shop, the Warehouse with its complete system of over-head runways for the speedy movement of goods; the facilities for packing, despatch and transport – these are only a selected list of departments which comprise the vast organisation of which Warrington is so justly proud.

Meanwhile Pearson & Knowles concentrated on supplying the construction industry, securing valuable contracts for the casting of bridge girders, locomotive wheels and axles as well as valves, tubes, tanks and castings.

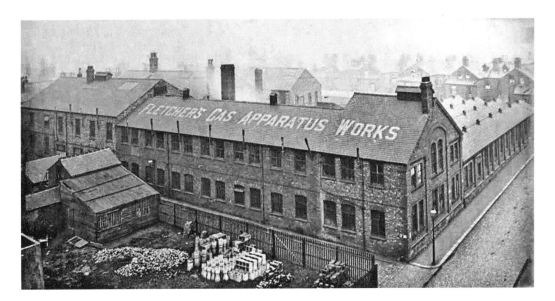

Above: Fletcher Russell & Co. grew out of an amalgamation in 1892 between the firms of Thomas Fletcher and Russell's iron foundry of Manchester, who made Fletcher's castings.

Right: Richmond's Academy Street foundry capitalized on the demand for smaller gas appliances to fit into the new middle-class homes that appeared in the late nineteenth century.

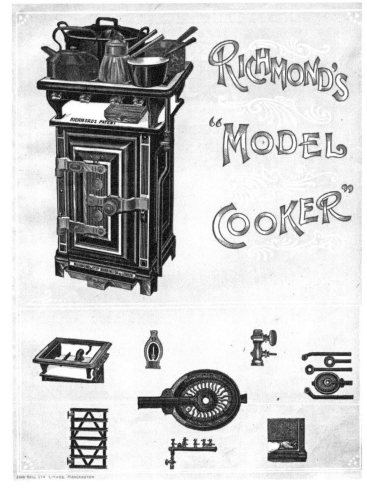

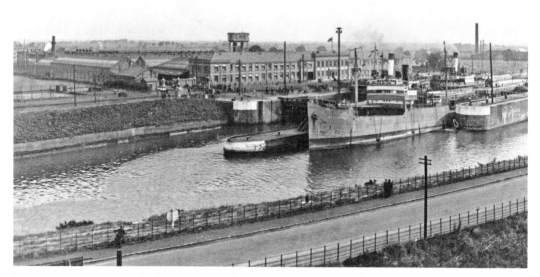

Richmond's new works by Latchford Locks on the Manchester Ship Canal was one of the largest of its kind in England.

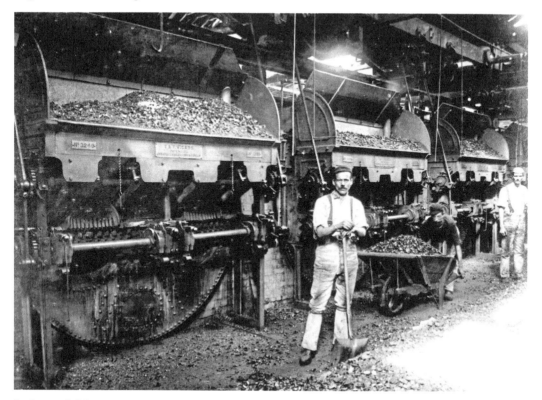

Richmond's labourers stoke the furnaces ready for the production of a wide range of cookers and gas appliances.

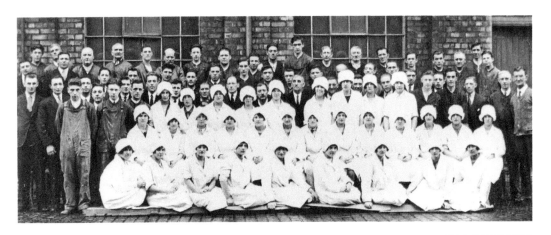

Above: The staff of Richmond's Chandos Department takes a break from enamelling gas cooker parts to pose for an official photograph in the 1920s.

Right: Richmond's trademark New World cookers celebrated liberation from the open hearth fire or cumbersome kitchen range.

Nos. 345/348

NEW WORLD COOKERS

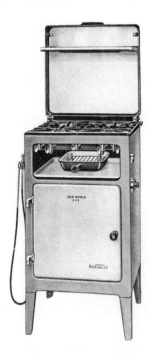

The New World No. 345 Cooker in green porcelain enamel finish, with "Regulo" oven-heat control. The illustration shows coverplate lifted and solid plate shelf in position.

Page 3

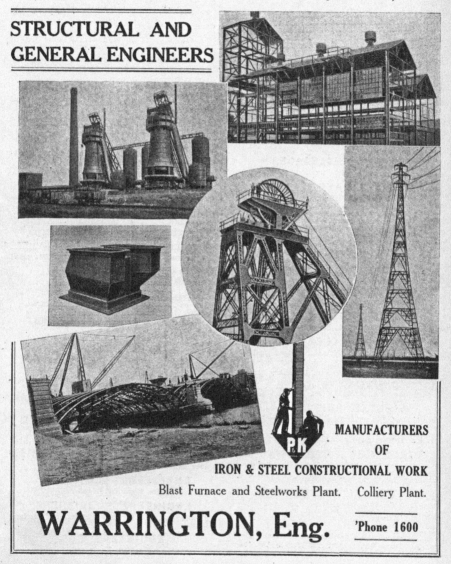

Bewsey-based Pearson & Knowles was formed by the amalgamation of three major local companies, including the Dallam Forge Co. in 1874. It later specialised in supplying large civil engineering projects.

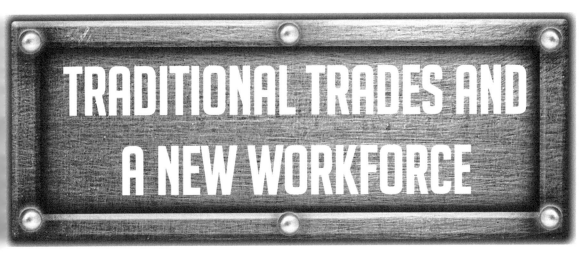

TRADITIONAL TRADES AND A NEW WORKFORCE

Although textiles and metalworking were major employers in the factory age the leather trade and brewing continued to flourish from the days when Warrington was primarily a market town in an agricultural rural landscape.

Tanning and leather working had been Warrington trades since the Middle Ages as a byproduct of the animals slaughtered at Warrington's meat market. By the late nineteenth century tanneries were concentrated around Winwick Road, Mersey Street, Howley, Latchford, Penketh and Orford.

Small-scale breweries were already well established in Warrington by the early seventeenth century, thanks to the pure local well water and ample supplies of grain to make the vital ingredient of malt. Brewing expanded rapidly from the late eighteenth century with the arrival of the Greenall dynasty, which not only brewed beer but later distilled gin and vodka. By the 1860s Greenall's were joined by rival brewers Walker & Son at Dallam Lane and the Burtonwood brewery.

From the mid-nineteenth century Warrington's businessmen also became active in politics, including brewers Gilbert Greenall and Sir Andrew Barclay Walker (seen here) and newspaper owner Alexander Mackie.

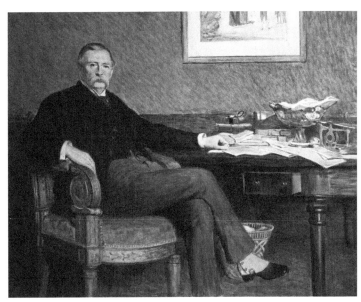

While the majority of Warrington's workers were employed in the town's many industries, by the 1891 census around 12 per cent of the town's workforce and a substantial proportion of women worked in the retail sector. By the early twentieth century new career opportunities were opening up to women as teachers, nursed and in clerical jobs.

A new workforce of professional classes was still largely male-dominated with increased numbers of bankers, lawyers, architects, doctors and public sector workers. Warrington also had a successor to Eyres' Press in Mackie's printing and newspaper empire.

TANNING AND BREWING

The 1891 census revealed that tanneries and the leather trade had become the town's third largest employer. Tannery labour was back-breaking and hazardous because of the chemicals involved, which also polluted the River Mersey, while the smells from the works hung over the town. By the late nineteenth century Warrington tanneries were thriving and imported animal hides from all over the world to be processed into products ranging from shoe leather to industrial belting. By the mid-twentieth century the tanning industry was largely unchanged but cheaper foreign imports soon formed a threat to the local tanneries survival.

Meanwhile local breweries had become more competitive with mechanisation. All three of Warrington's main brewery chains also tried to safeguard their market by establishing a wide network of pubs that were tied to only supplying their brewery owner's beer. Greenalls built up one of the largest number of licensed houses in Lancashire, Cheshire, North Wales, Shropshire, Staffordshire and other areas as well as the majority of the hotels and inns in Warrington. However, it was their main rival brewer that became known for their 'Walker's Warrington Ales'.

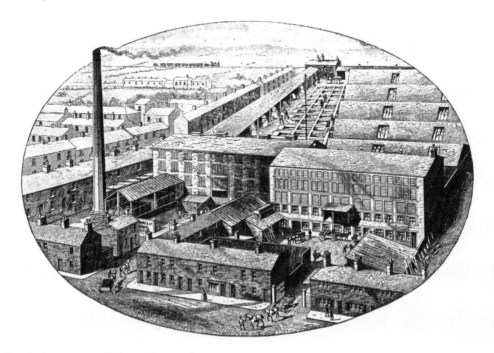

Fleming's tannery off Fennel Street shows a typical layout with a grid of small tan pits and tall drying sheds where the treated hides would be hung.

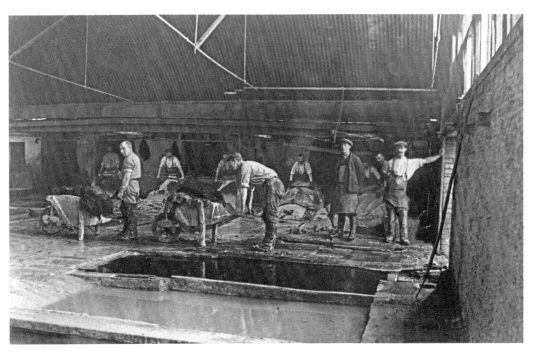

Tannery work was hazardous: men could slip and drown in the corrosive contents of these deep tan pits while anthrax could be contracted from spores carried on the hides.

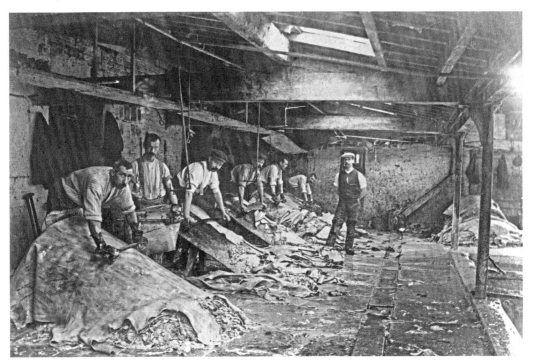

Once the dry hides had been softened in the lime pits the hair was skilfully shaved off over the fleshing beams by hand with a curved fleshing knife.

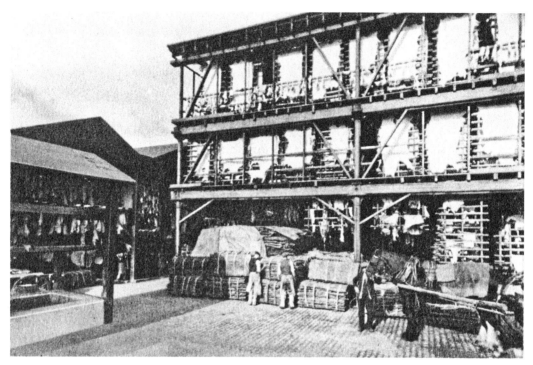

After the hides had been treated and dried they were hung in the drying sheds, which had louvred windows.

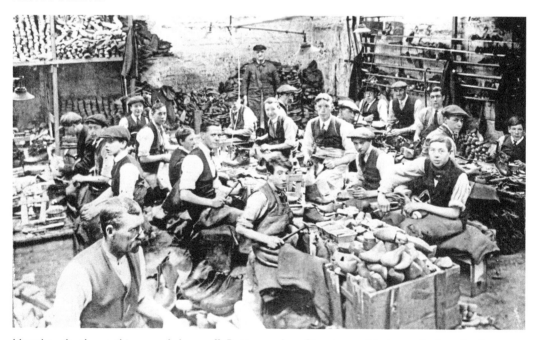

Houghton's clog-making workshop off Buttermarket Street provided sturdy long-lasting protective footwear. The clatter of wooden soles on cobblestones and sparks from clog irons were a traditional part of working life.

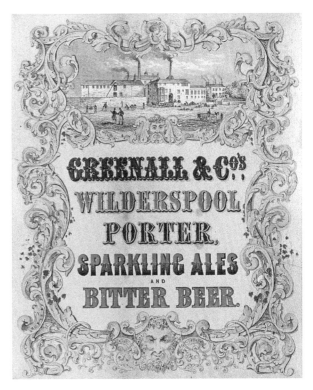

Right: Greenall's original Wilderspool brewery site included the family home of the White House (far right). Later it became the company headquarters when Gilbert Greenall moved to Walton Hall.

Below: In 1761 Thomas Dakin purchased this distillery in Bridge Street and began producing London Dry Gin. A century later Greenall's took over to trade as G & J Greenall.

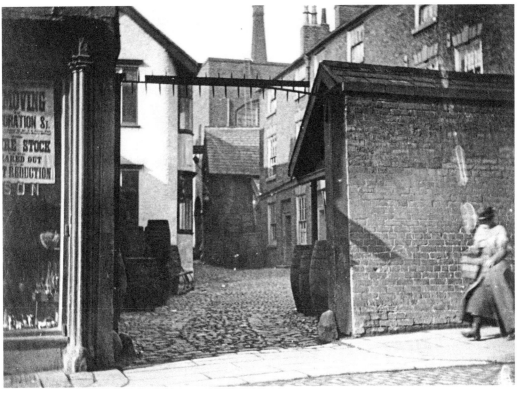

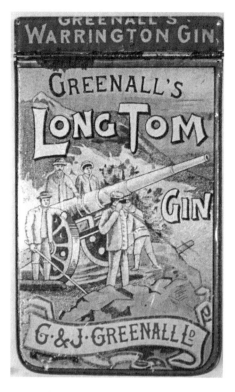

Left: While Greenall's continued to make Dakin's original botanical gin to its secret recipe, they also introduced new brands.

Below: By the early 1900s the Wilderspool brewery had been completely rebuilt and housed modern equipment, an extensive hop stores, a new bottling stores and cooperage works, yards and offices.

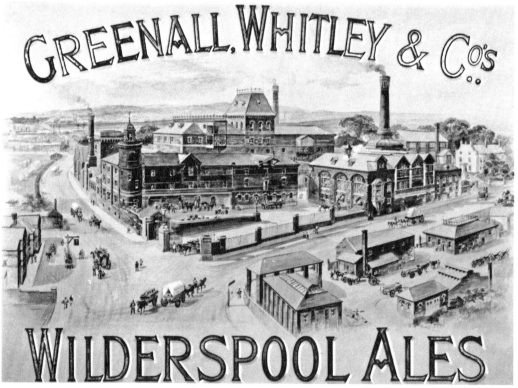

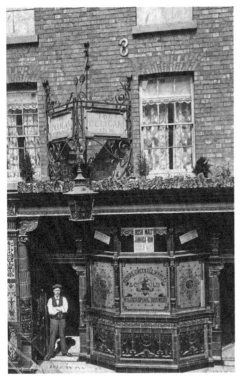

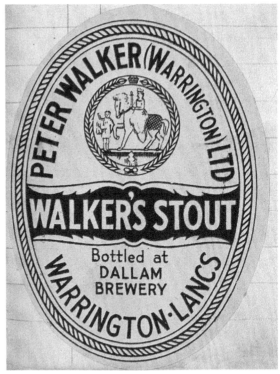

Above left: The Pelican Inn in Buttermarket Street was typical of the elaborate pub architecture favoured by Greenalls in the early 1900s.

Above Right: Walker & Son took over the King Street brewery in 1846 before setting up headquarters in Dallam Lane to sell their 'Walker's Warrington Ales'.

Right: Sir Gilbert Greenall who also served as Warrington's MP and lived at Walton Hall.

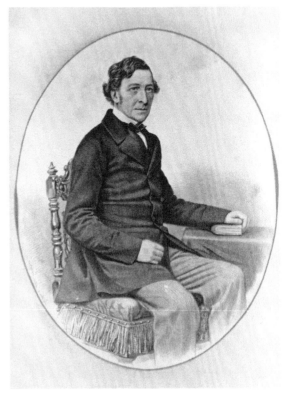

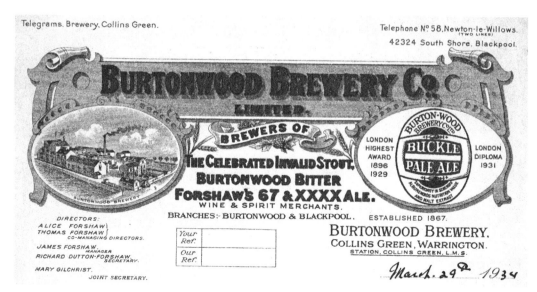

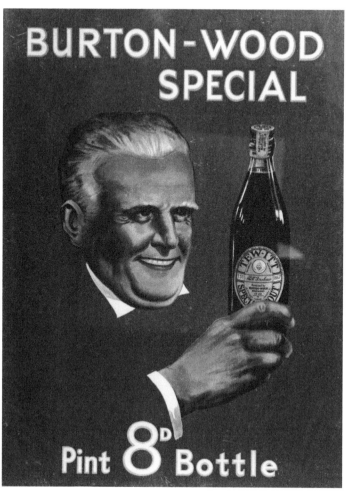

Above: Burtonwood became home to Warrington's third major brewery in 1867 when the Forshaw family set up a brewery there.

Left: Burtonwood brewery remained a family concern, building up a large chain of tied pubs and introducing bottled beer as early as 1895.

RETAILING AND THE PROFESSIONAL SECTOR

By the early 1900s the town's centuries' old market flourished and local trade directories of the period list a wide range of small shopkeepers, from local corner shops to the larger specialist retailers, which began to occupy the town centre's four mains streets. By its centenary in 1960 the Co-op was an important employer with twenty-five shops around the town. By the 1980s some of its smaller branches closed while other familiar grocery chains like Milling's and Melias' also disappeared from the high street with the advent of national supermarkets.

Although vast numbers of women still worked in domestic service and many men were poorly paid labourers, twentieth-century Warrington saw the beginnings of a new workforce who did not work on the factory floor. Medicine was accepted as a profession. There was a rigid hierarchy on the wards, from the doctor to the matron, who ruled with a rod of iron, to ward sisters and finally the ordinary nurses.

Public services also became a major employer, with increased numbers working in the police force and fire service, as well as postmen, council workers and the utility sector.

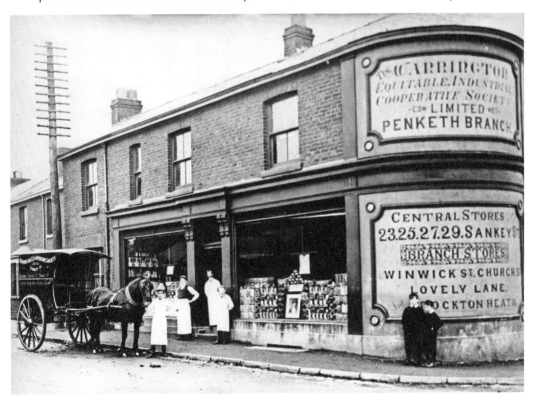

Founded in 1860, the Warrington Co-operative society aimed to supply unadulterated goods at fair prices and returned a proportion of the profits to the society's members in a cash dividend.

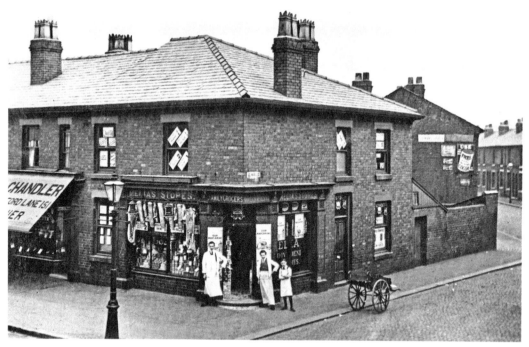

Melia's corner shop in Orford Lane was a typical grocery store prior to supermarkets, with counter service from the manager and his assistant and delivery by the errand boy.

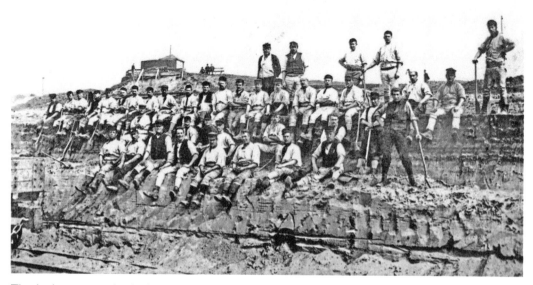

The Irish navvies who built the Manchester Ship Canal were resented by local workers as foreigners who would work for low wages and accept poor conditions.

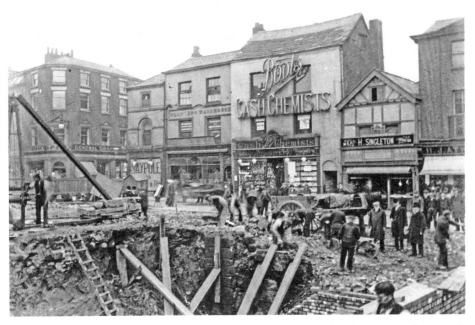

Between 1900 and 1915 a large-scale redevelopment of Bridge Street saw the town's main thoroughfare swarming with builders with little regard for today's health and safety concerns.

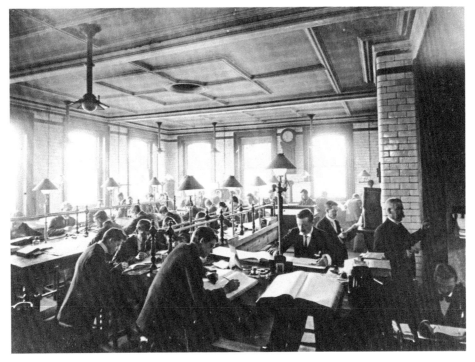

By the early twentieth century white-collar workers like these invoice ledger clerks were beginning to appear in the offices of Warrington's expanding businesses.

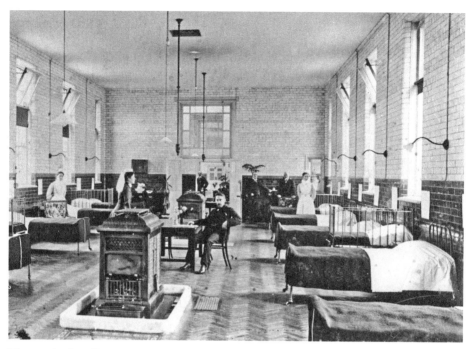

The medical staff in the stark ward of Warrington Fever hospital in Aikin Street stands ready to receive isolation cases.

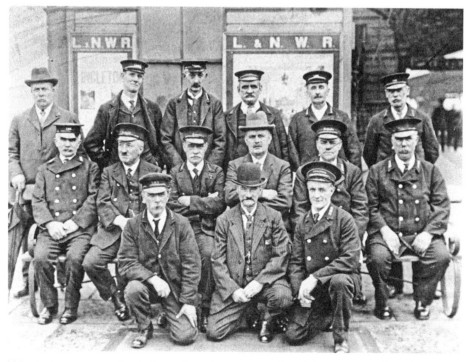

Warrington was a major hub on the railway network and its station staff took pride in their status in the community.

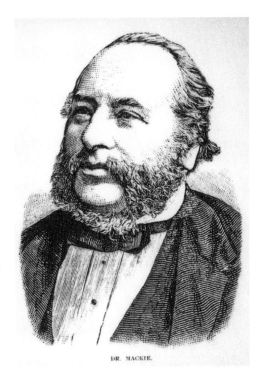

DR. MACKIE.

Right: Alexander Mackie launched the *Warrington Guardian* series of weekly newspapers in 1853. Inspired by the radical *Manchester Guardian*, his paper had the masthead 'Neutral in all matters Political and Religious'.

Below: By 1880 Mackie's newspaper empire had expanded across the country and his new Warrington headquarters in Sankey Street proudly faced the Town Hall.

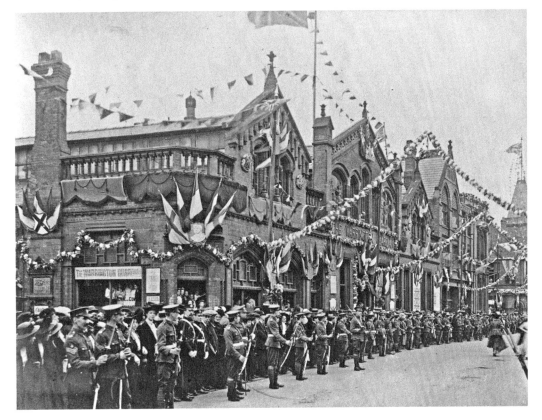

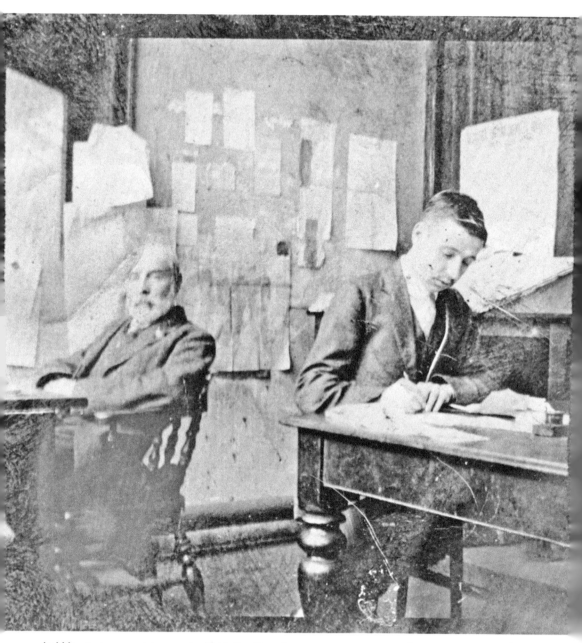

As Warrington went to war in 1914 the *Guardian* reporters were ready to cover events for the twice weekly editions without today's instant communications.

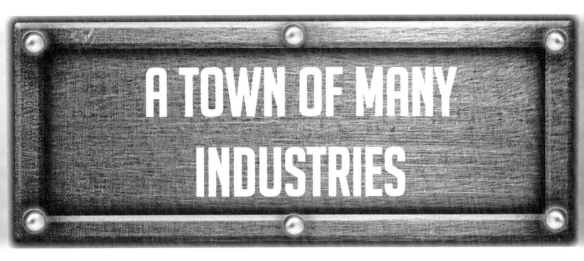

A TOWN OF MANY INDUSTRIES

In the years before the outbreak of the First World War in 1914 Britain was gripped by industrial unrest but escaped the worst depravation because of the diversity of its industrial base. *Livelihood and Poverty* surveyed the town in September 1913 and recorded that:

There are in Warrington some of the largest ironworks in the United Kingdom. There are also several wireworks where the processes of wire drawing and weaving are carried out. Firms manufacturing bedsteads, tubes, boilers and engines, and two of the largest gas-stove works in the country are established there. A well-known firm of soap manufacturers employs a large number of persons. In addition there are tanneries and breweries. Other important trades are those in boxes, printing, glass, rubber, flour, white lead, timber and building materials. With so many industries upon which it is dependent, the town escapes comparatively lightly when one or a few of its trades are suffering from commercial depression or the effects of a strike.

This economic resilience helped Warrington survive the economic depression of the late 1920s to early 1930s and ensured that the town's industries played a vital role in both twentieth-century world wars.

A second major quayside, known as Bishop's Wharf, developed near to Warrington Bridge to serve the industries at Howley. In 1933 the *Warrington Examiner* hailed Bishop's Wharf as 'Prosperity Corner'.

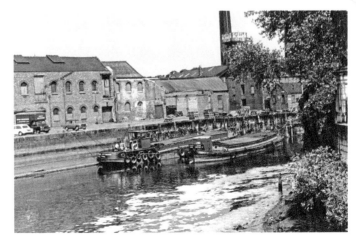

By the 1970s Warrington was no longer immune to worldwide economic trends or industrial unrest against the impact of the Conservative government's restrictive trade union legislation of the 1980s. However, unlike many of its neighbours Warrington emerged into the twenty-first century in a stronger economic position, even though the town's industrial landscape was irreversibly changed.

WARRINGTON'S INDUSTRIES AT WAR

During the First World War Warrington's heavy industries such as the iron, steel and wire works were crucial to supplying armaments, torpedo nets and, above all, barbed wire needed for trench warfare. Ninety per cent of the output of Armitage & Rigby's Cockhedge cotton mill was for military usage, ranging from bandages to khaki drill cloth. Crosfield's produced glycerine, which was vital to the manufacture of ammunition.

During the Second World War Warrington's wireworks produced items ranging from tank suspensions to wire mesh for gas masks. Cardboard boxes for gas masks and Red Cross parcels were produced at the town's box works. Crosfield's engineering shop was involved in munitions work, which had little to do with the production of the firm's famous soaps.

In peacetime new businesses such as British Aluminium and Thames Board Mills had come to Warrington while established firms had begun to mechanise and embraced the motor age. Less welcome for some employers was the growth of unionised labour and what they regarded as associated restrictive practices. All of Warrington's industries would be tested by the industrial climate of the second half of the twentieth century and only the most resilient would survive.

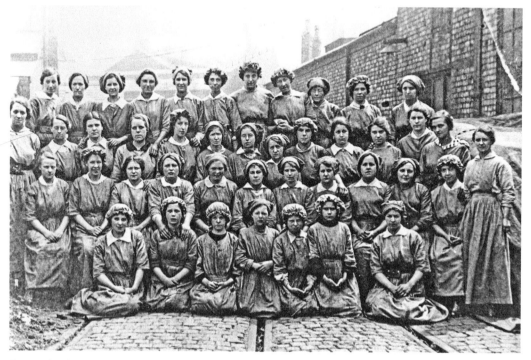

During both world wars of the twentieth century women tackled heavy jobs normally done by men but job opportunities and equal pay in peacetime were harder to achieve.

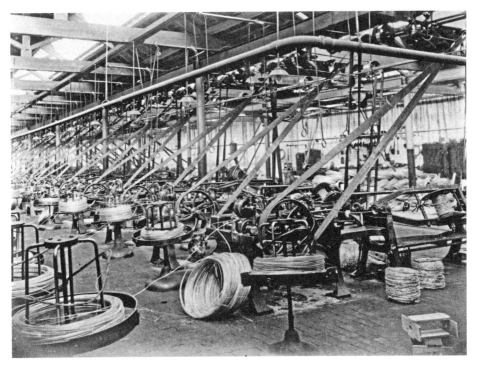

Rylands' barbed-wire department served a growing agricultural market in Britain and supplied the battlefields and trenches during the First World War.

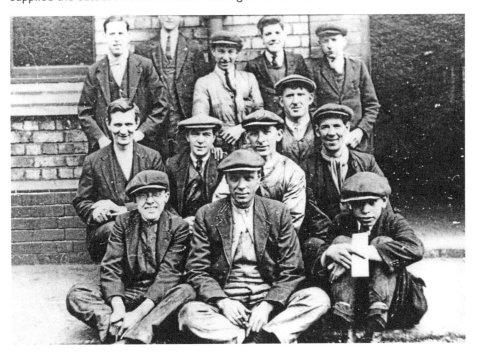

A Firth Co. apprentice proudly holds up his apprenticeship papers in the early 1920s. Even an apprenticeship did not guarantee of job in the economic depression of the 1930s.

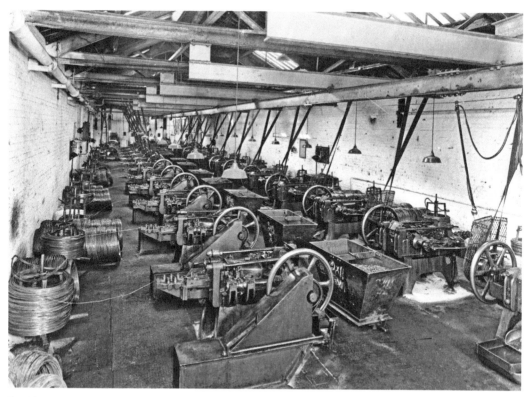

By 1940 Ryland's probably had the largest modern nail-making factory in the world with a total weekly production running into hundreds of tons.

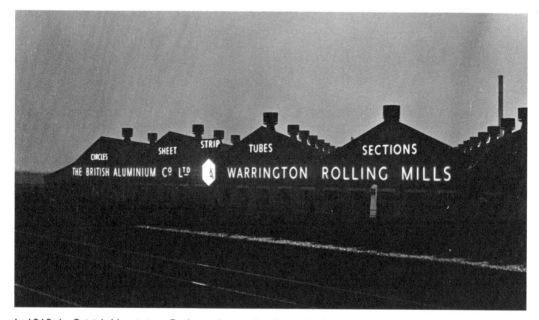

In 1913 the British Aluminium Co. brought another branch of the metal industry to Warrington at their Bank Quay plant. This new lightweight metal used traditional metalworking techniques.

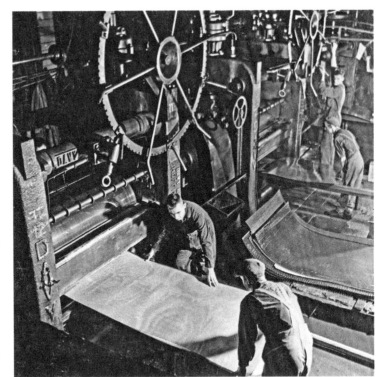

The process of sheet rolling aluminium was very labour-intensive but working conditions were better than those employed in similar tasks in older iron mills.

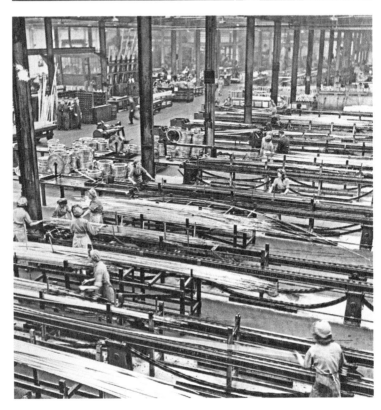

In this 1946 photograph women are hard at work at British Aluminium's draw benches, which pulled out the metal through dies to the required shape.

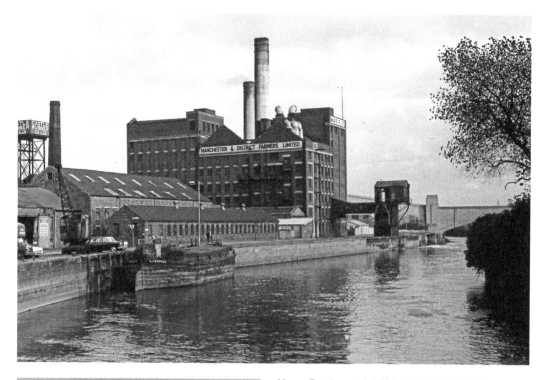

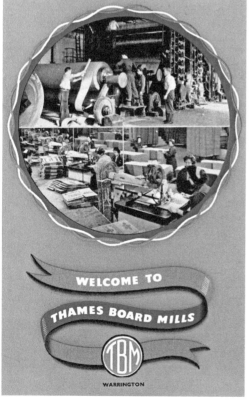

Above: By the mid-1930s Bishop's Wharf was home to Howley Power Station, Manchester & District Farmers and the Castle Rubber Co., as well as the Bishop Wharf Carrying Co.

Left: In 1936, Thames Board Mills expanded their operation from Purfleet in Essex by opening its huge purpose-built factory at Arpley and creating almost 300 new jobs locally.

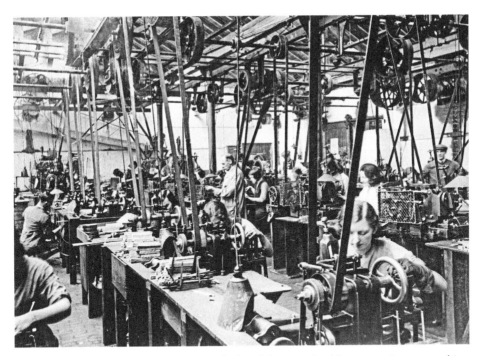

By the mid-1930s Stubs switched the whole of their toolmaking operation to machine cutting, also employing women on the work benches.

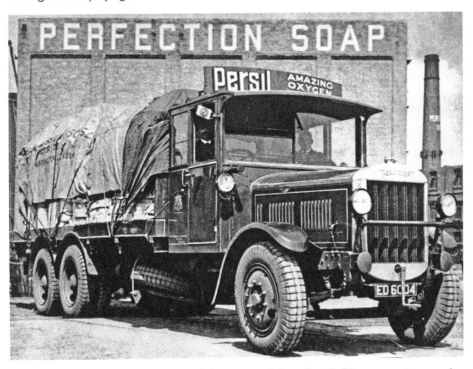

Crosfield's had a fleet of Thornycroft lorries to deliver Persil, Glitto scouring powder and the famous Pinkobolic soap to customers far and wide.

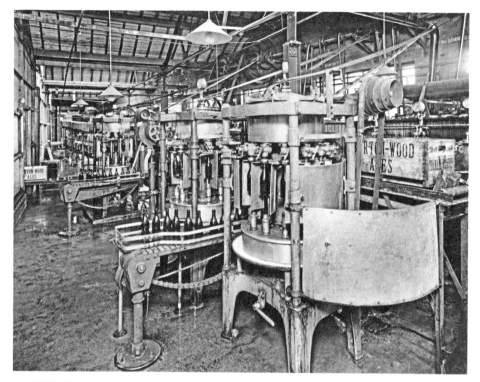

In 1937, Burtonwood brewery was substantially rebuilt and modernised while mechanisation helped to meet the growing demands for its beers.

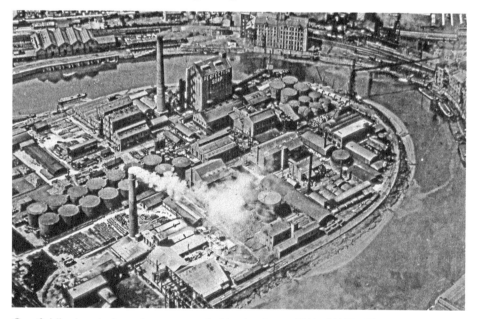

Crosfield's chemical products were vital in the Second World War. They were used in camouflage paint and searchlights, while sulphite soaps protected against dermatitis in the explosives and filling factories.

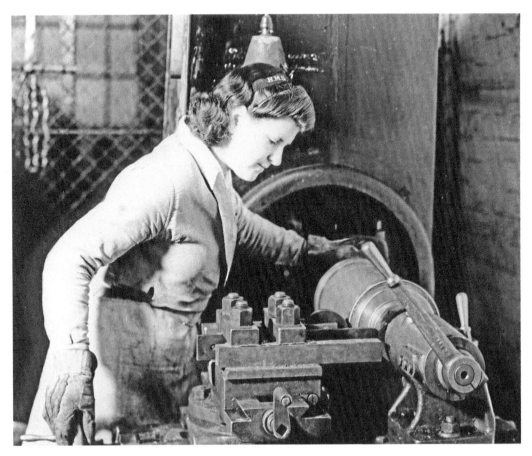

Above: During the First and Second world wars Warrington's factories were diverted to war work with the wire works and foundries playing a vital role.

Right: Fletcher Russell's Wilderspool Causeway workers are seen here in the production of shells while the town's wire works made everything from tank suspensions to wire mesh for gas masks.

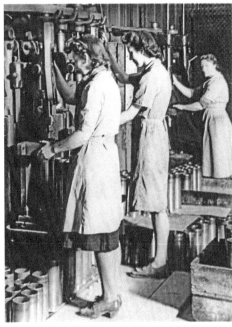

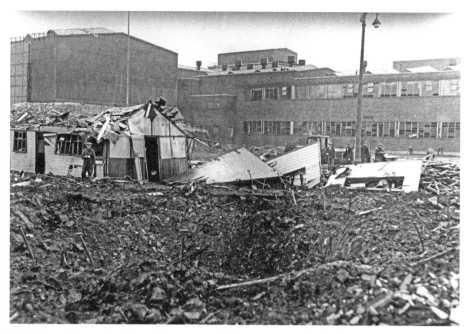

Warrington's wartime factories attracted German air raids. On Saturday 14 September a fête at Thames Board Mill's recreation ground was bombed, allegedly mistaken for the adjacent British Aluminium works.

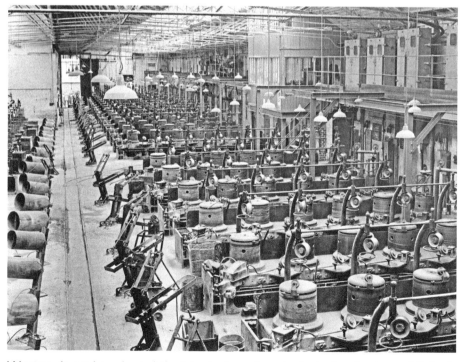

Wartime demand accelerated the introduction of mechanised wire drawing and Ryland's opened the '41 Continuous Mill in Battersby Lane in 1941, with a weekly output of 1,500 tons.

THE END OF AN ERA

By the 1960s the world was emerging from post-war austerity to become a more global society. Technology was beginning to change the way people lived and Warrington's industries needed to adapt to survive. Some occupations and smaller craft-based businesses disappeared. Synthetic materials and cheaper foreign imports led to the demise of long-established trades such as leather and textiles.

However, Warrington's chemical industries were more resilient as their products were adaptable to emerging markets. The town's heavy metal works were hardest hit and even Warrington's rugby league team was renamed as the wire industry declined in importance.

Nationally or internationally owned businesses were less concerned by the impact of their restructure proposals on Warrington than overall profitability. Bewsey found itself at the centre of a bitter industrial dispute with a prolonged strike at Greening's wire works in 1983 when a management decision to axe eighty-nine jobs led to mass picketing and a prolonged strike. *Warrington Guardian* headlines of the day reported the unfolding of over thirteen weeks of strike action but ironically their photographic archive of events was lost under their new owner, Eddy Shah, who became embroiled in an even longer dispute over the introduction of new technology and non-unionised labour.

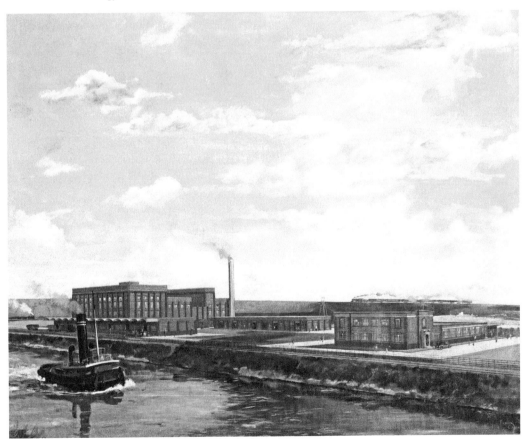

In March 1950 Laporte Chemicals opened the Baronet Works on the banks of the Manchester Ship Canal at Lower Walton. Warrington's second chemical plant produced hydrogen peroxide.

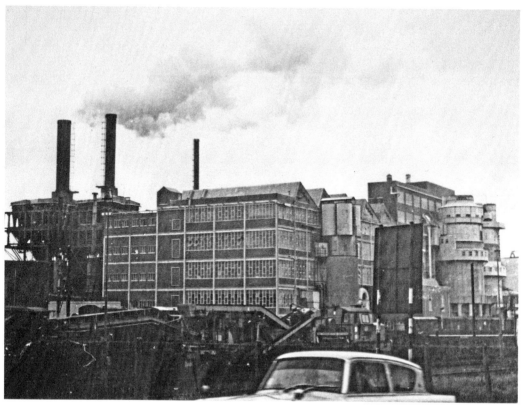

In peacetime Unilever resumed normal production. The smell of soap hung over the town centre once again and foam from the plant appeared upriver by Bishop's Wharf.

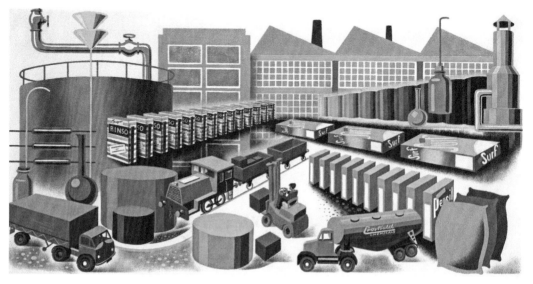

In the post-war years Unilever introduced new machinery to its detergent production lines and brightly coloured packets of Persil, Surf and Rinso rolled off the conveyor belts for despatch.

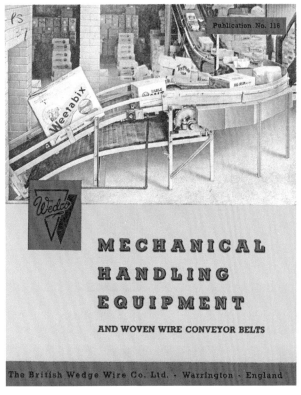

Right: A trade catalogue from the British Wedge Wire Co., which supplied other heavy industries and thus suffered from their decline.

Below: In the post-war period Ryland's trademark Rylink wire fencing became one of the firm's success stories and large-scale machinery was brought in to expand production.

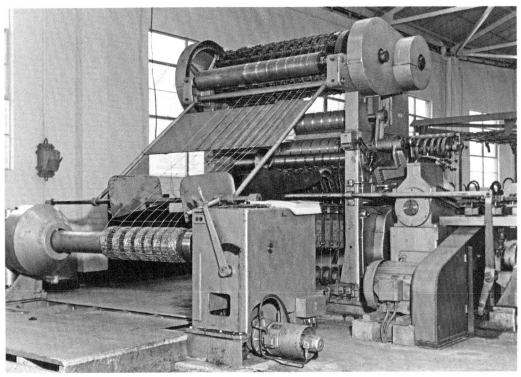

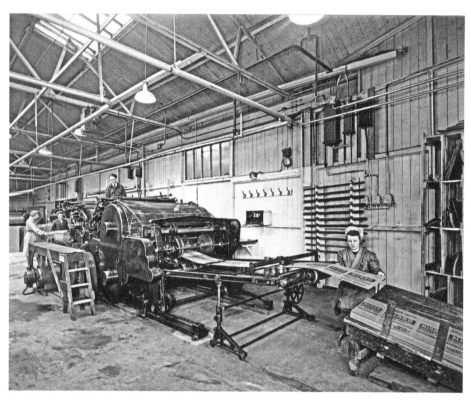

By the late 1940s the Alliance Box works on Orford Lane also embraced large-scale machinery in the printing and folding of its cardboard cartons.

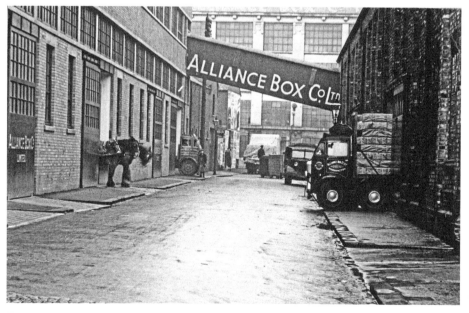

The Alliance Box works on Orford Lane flourished in the mid-twentieth century manufacturing fancy and cardboard boxes for firms like Jacob's biscuits of Liverpool.

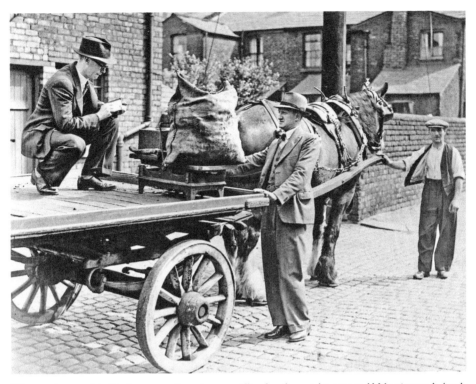

The coalman with his horse and cart was still a familiar sight around Warrington's back streets in the 1950s before clean-air legislation led to alternative forms of domestic heating.

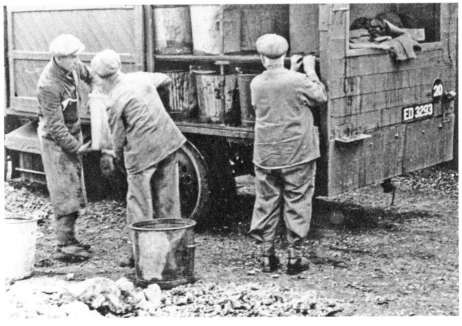

The 'night soil' men performed one of the least enviable jobs in Warrington until the 1950s by removing the personal waste of the town's population who lacked flushing toilets.

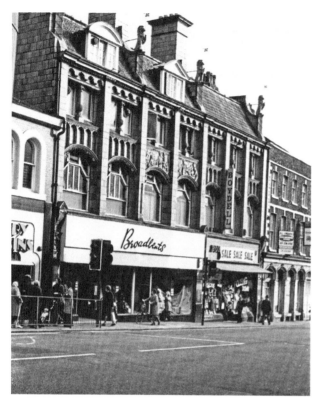

By the late 1970s most of Warrington's family-owned department stores like Broadbent and Turner's had disappeared from the town's main streets and jobs for milliners and drapers disappeared with them.

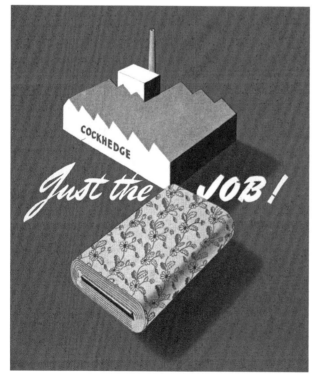

Foreign competition from Britain's former colonies led to the closure of Cockhedge's spinning mill in the 1960s. The main four-storey building was sold but weaving new types of materials continued.

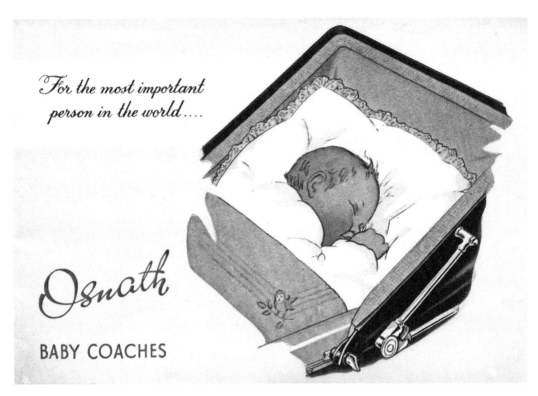

*For the most important
person in the world....*

Osnath

BABY COACHES

Above: In 1965 the Osnath Co. ceased production of their sturdy traditional prams at their Lythgoes Lane works. Modern women wanted lightweight pushchairs to fold up into the family car.

Right: Whittle Bros Mersey Street tannery survived until the late twentieth century but even demand for their patented leather belting to drive machinery could not ensure their survival.

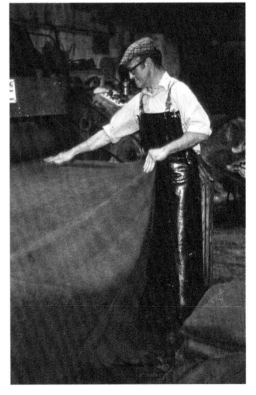

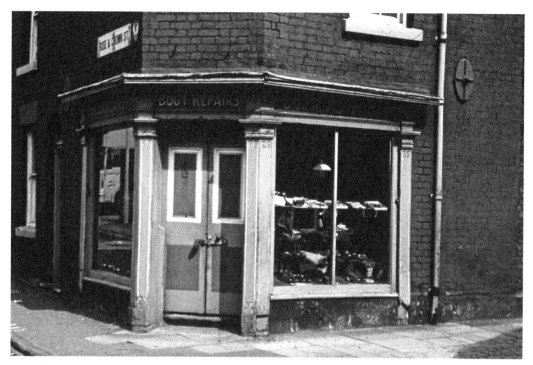

The availability of cheap imported shoes with synthetic soles hastened the closure of Douglas Gandy's clog shop in Mersey Street in the 1970s and marked the end of an era.

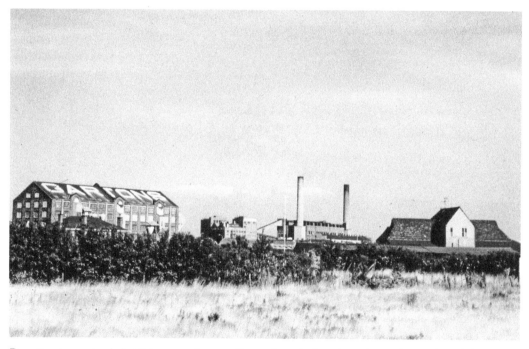

Despite pioneering hybridising cereal crops Garton's agricultural seed merchants closed their Arpley headquarters in 1983 and another century-old business ended.

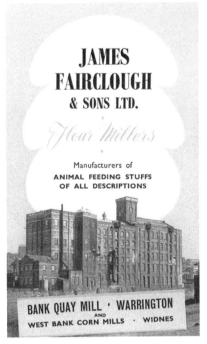

JAMES FAIRCLOUGH & SONS LTD.

Flour Millers

Manufacturers of
**ANIMAL FEEDING STUFFS
OF ALL DESCRIPTIONS**

BANK QUAY MILL · WARRINGTON
AND
WEST BANK CORN MILLS · WIDNES

Right: After the closure of Scott's bakery in Liverpool in 1984 the main market for the former Fairclough's Bank Quay flour disappeared and the mill closed.

Below: Production of the *Warrington Guardian* in the 1960s was hardly changed since founder Alexander Mackie's time. Newspapers were a closed shop to non-union labour and typesetting a skilled job.

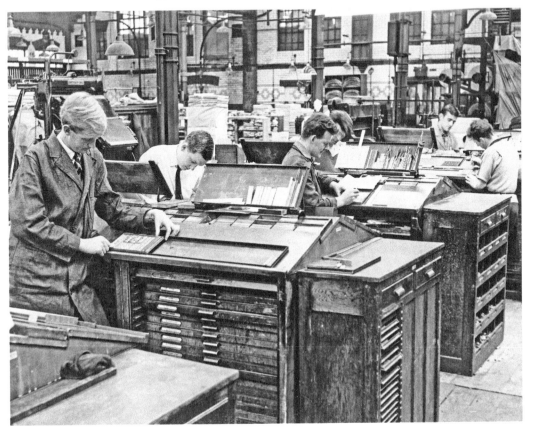

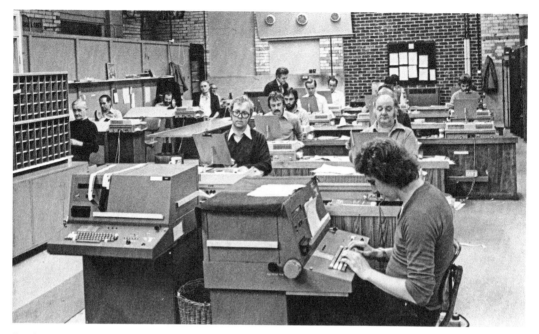

By the time the *Warrington Guardian* celebrated its 125th birthday in 1978 linotype had given way to the latest electronic typesetting equipment.

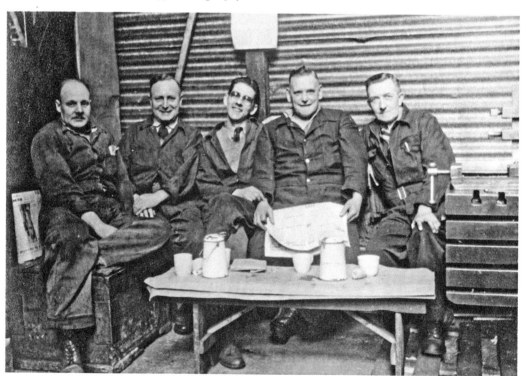

Greening's workmen enjoy a tea break in 1957 with Wilf Briggs (welder) second from right and Stan Mottram (fitter) far right.

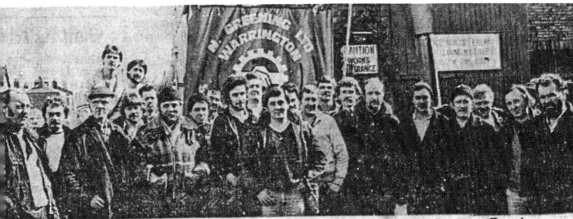

The Greenings strikers picket the factory's main gates in Bewsey Road.

Bewsey found itself at the centre of Warrington's most bitter industrial disputes with a prolonged strike at Greening's Wire Works in 1983.

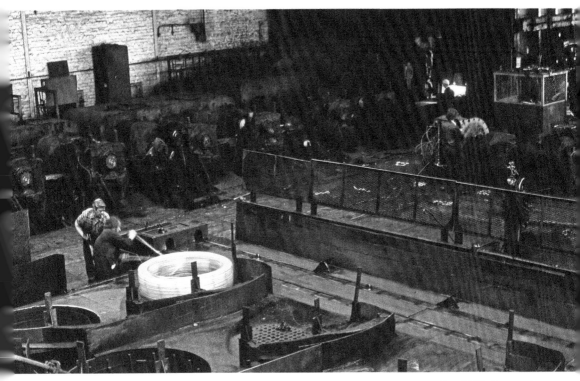

As the coil of white-hot metal cooled at Lancashire Steel's Rod and Bar Mill in 1980 the works was also in its dying days.

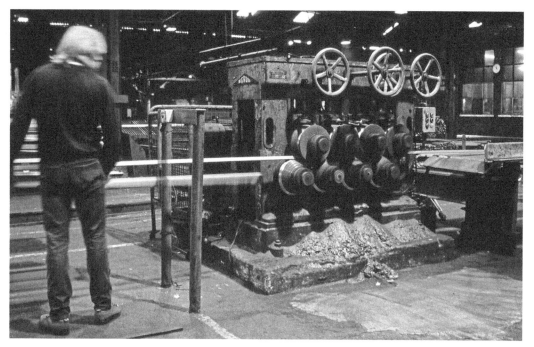

The changing world economic climate of the 1980s and 1990s led to the closure of most of Warrington's heavy industry with wire, iron and steel production hardest hit.

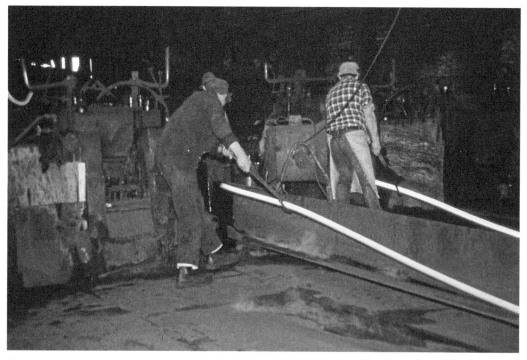

The last billet of steel rolled out of No. 4 Mill at Monks Hall in March 1986 and the era of Warrington's heavy metal trade was over.

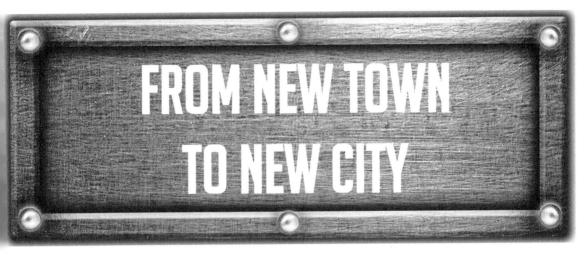

FROM NEW TOWN TO NEW CITY

As Warrington emerged from the national industrial decline of the 1980s a *Sunday Times* article of 1990 saw it as a town in transition:

> There is still pink froth on the Mersey in Warrington, Cheshire, and smoke belches from factory chimneys but the future of this town lies in its landscaped science park, where high-tech companies are flourishing. Warrington is one of 30 places named by the Henley Centre for Forecasting as the boom towns of the 1990s … Warrington, designated as a New Town in 1968, struggled as a manufacturing base. Now that it has diversified into white-collar jobs it is prospering.

During the turbulent period of the 1970s and 1980s Warrington had seen the closure of long-established local businesses while globalisation of the financial markets saw national firms that had bases in the town rationalise their operations and close their Warrington branches.

Warrington's position on the national motorway network has been key to its success in attracting investment from national and international businesses.

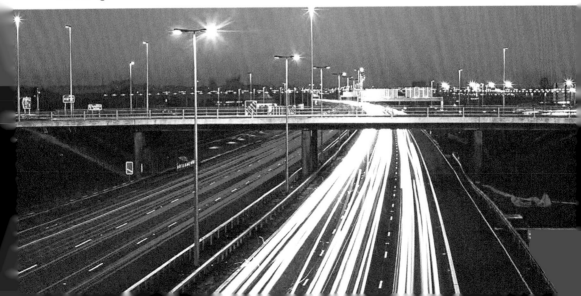

Even employment sectors such as the railways restructured their operations and cut their workforce.

Warrington's diverse economy helped it escape the fate of many one-industry towns and its location and connectivity remained crucial to the New Town Development Plan and Warrington Borough Council's 'Warrington Means Business City Centre Master Plan of 2017'. This articulates the vision for its future of a city with a population that has trebled since 1968:

> Warrington is one of the most economically successful towns in the UK today. Its future is assured by its wonderful location and connectivity, the entrepreneurial character of its people and businesses, its attractiveness to investors and its cultural offer.

THE NEW TOWN ERA

Warrington's designation as a new town on 26 April 1968 was partly to solve its post-war legacy of former military bases at Risley and Padgate and the expected closure of Burtonwood air base. Warrington was felt to be strategically placed to develop as an economic centre for south-east Lancashire and north-east Cheshire. The town's population was expected to rise from around 65,000 to 200,000 by 1991, encouraged by the development of new employment opportunities.

Crucial to the plan's success was the town's connectivity with the new motorway network, its continued railway and ship canal freight links and, latterly, two regional airports. New business parks were connected to the regional and national transport infrastructure by a series of urban motorways.

Midway through the implementation of the plan Warrington saw many of its traditional industries disappear. The wire and steel industries succumbed to rationalisation caused by new cheaper foreign competition and changing working practices. Overcapacity in the brewing industry and regulations against the practice of tied houses saw the town's two major breweries close. The New Town Development Corporation was dissolved prematurely on 30 September 1989 and responsibility for Warrington's twenty-first-century economic development ultimately devolved to the council.

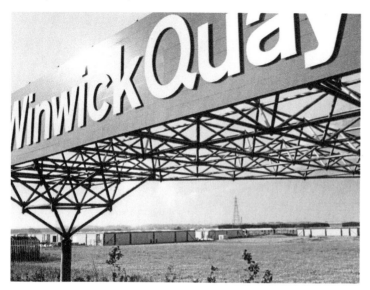

Winwick Quay was an early industrial estate developed under the New Town plans. Its location parallels the workshops of Roman Warrington at Wilderspool also alongside the A49 centuries earlier.

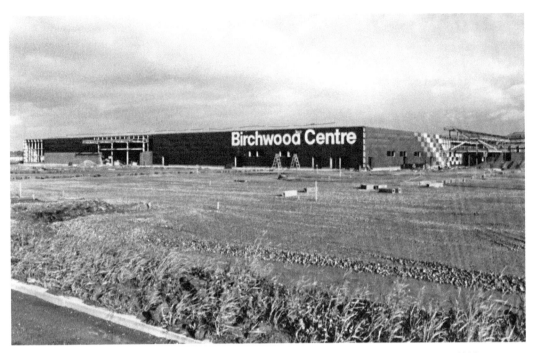

The Birchwood Centre was at the heart of a new community on the east of Warrington, created as part of the New Town vision for the derelict Risley Munitions Factory.

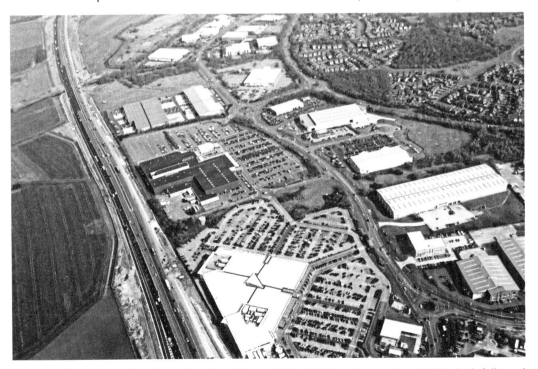

The Gemini retail park was developed alongside the M62 motorway (seen left), which followed the line of the runway of the disused Burtonwood Airbase.

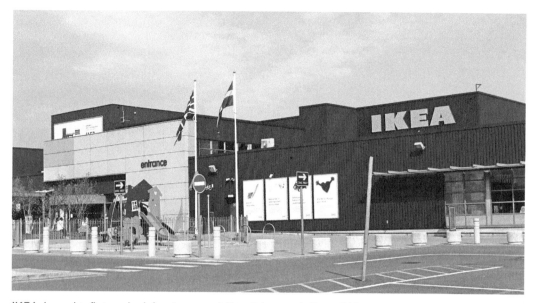

IKEA brought flat-packed furniture and Swedish meatballs to Warrington when it opened its first UK branch at Gemini in October 1987, and the superstore soon became a regional attraction.

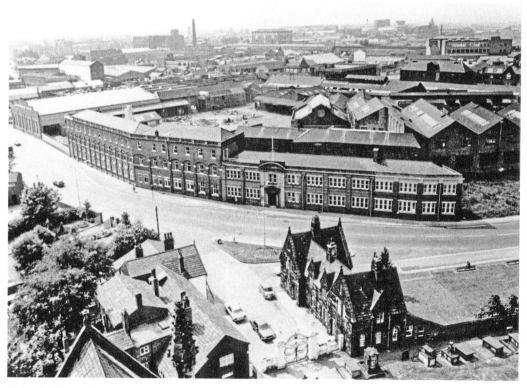

Ryland's Church Street and Dalton Banks works stretched for almost a third of a mile from Church Street to the Cheshire Lines railway in the background.

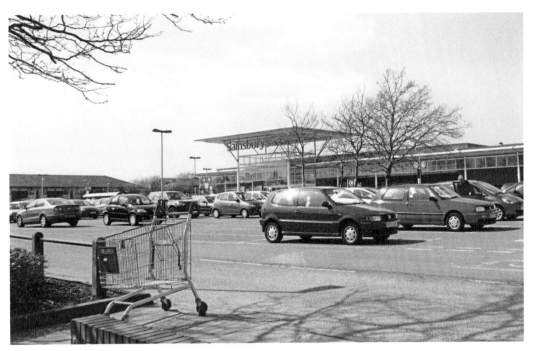

The closure of Ryland's Church Street works in the 1980s made the site available for Sainsbury's, who were looking to expand their supermarket operations in the north.

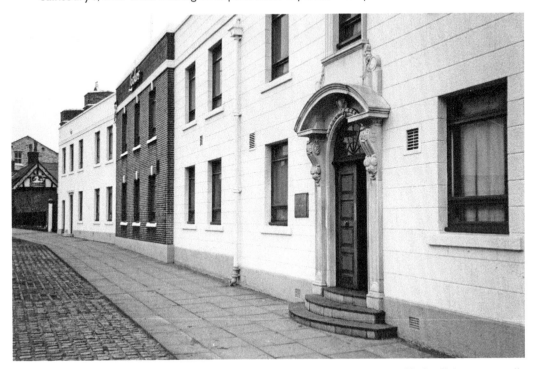

Locker's retained their Church Street headquarters after the demise of Ryland's but eventually relocated to a smaller unit and sold the site for housing development.

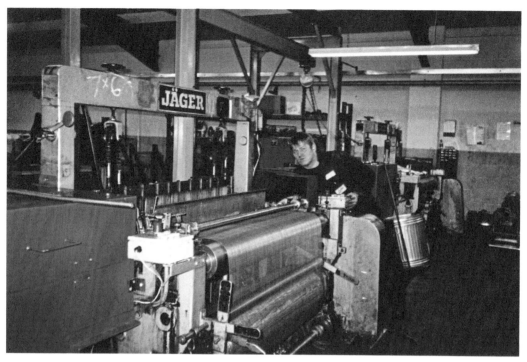

By the twenty-first century Lockers had adapted to produce mesh fine enough to be found in the filters of car engines or protecting automated cash machines.

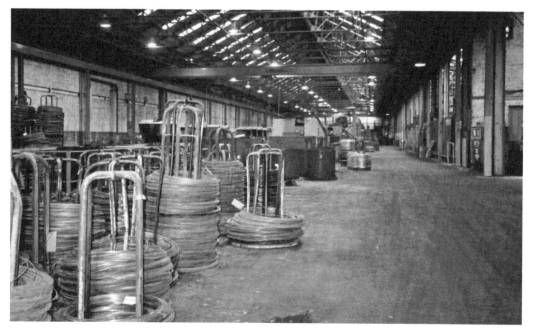

Carrington's ended production at Ryland's former Battersby Lane site in 2013 when housing development seemed more lucrative than producing steel wire in competition with cheaper foreign suppliers.

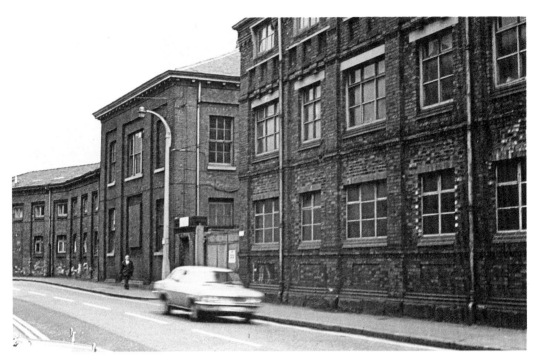

Above: By the early 1980s Stubs'
former toolmaking complex at
Cockhedge was ripe for development
but the New Town plan did not
favour industry located in the
town centre.

Right: In 1984 Charterhall properties
developed the former Stubs works
and Cockhedge Mill as a shopping
centre. Roof girders salvaged from
the old weaving sheds became a
feature in the mall.

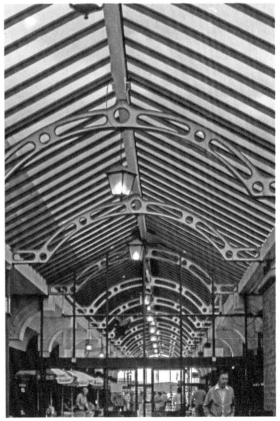

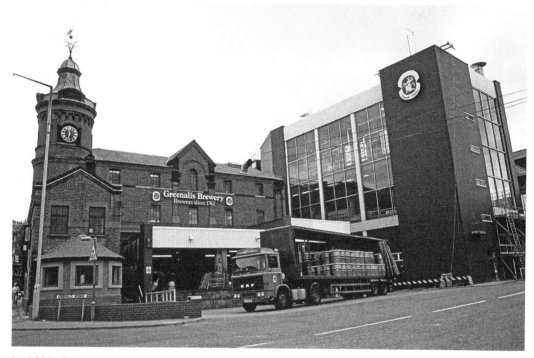

In 1990 Greenalls called last orders on their brewing operation at Wilderspool and the site was developed as Morrison's supermarket and business park, but the distinctive clock tower survived.

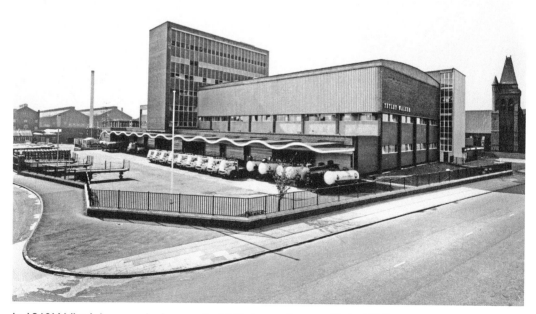

In 1960 Walker's brewery had merged with Tetleys to become Tetley Walker and the new firm rebuilt the Dallam Lane brewery in 1967.

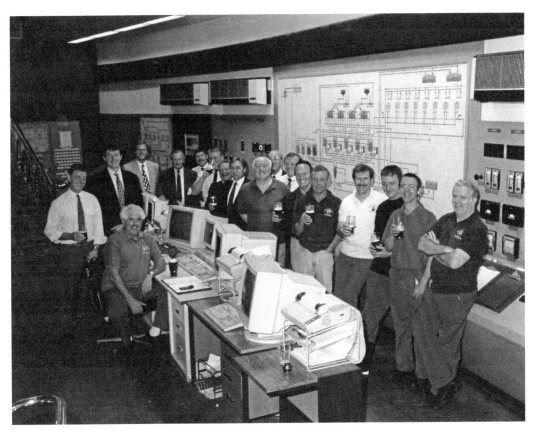

Even investment in an automated control room capable of producing six million barrels of beer a week with three staff was not enough to save Tetley Walker's from closure in 1996.

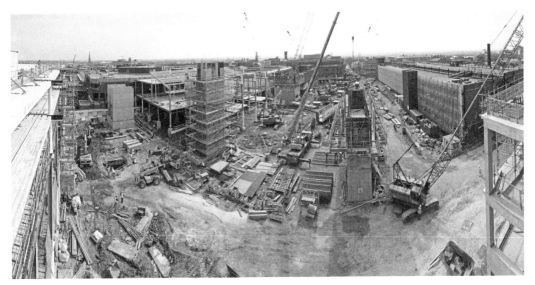

Between 1980 and 2007 a new shopping centre was created at Golden Square to continue Warrington's retail tradition and the Old Market Square became its centrepiece.

WARRINGTON MEANS BUSINESS

The 2016 Centre for Cities report ranked Warrington in its top ten locations best placed to drive national economic growth, with the largest sector of nuclear sector businesses in the UK primarily located on its business parks.

A 2015 report recognised Warrington's role as a centre for new technologies, naming it as a UK top-ten town for small and medium digital, creative and professional services. The town also has strengths in a range of other service activities including telecommunications, office administration and building.

The town ranks as number one out of sixty cities for the highest percentage of employment per population with 79.8 per cent of its population in employment. Warrington is also investing in developing a skilled future workforce with 98 per cent of sixteen–seventeen year olds in education or training, the second highest in the UK.

Some traditional businesses have adapted to prosper, notably the chemical industry. Smaller-scale wire weaving, brewing and even toolmaking trade provide links to the town's industrial heritage. The *Warrington Guardian* still chronicles the town's development, although instant online reporting via smart phones has revolutionised their work. Twenty-first-century Warrington is poised to adapt from 'A Town of Many Industries' to one that means business.

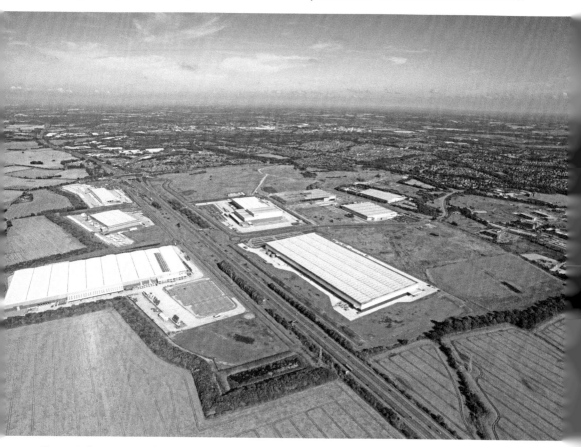

Omega's location on both sides of Junction 8 of the M62 was created as a logistics hub attractive to major national and international distribution companies.

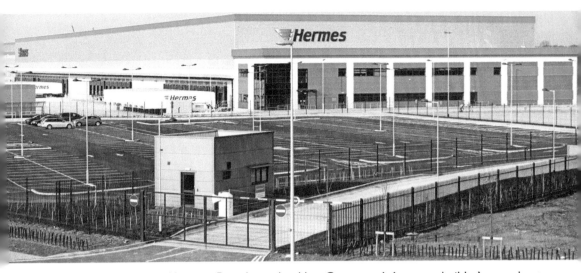

Major online giants Hermes Parcelnet, the Hut Group and Amazon, builder's merchant Travis Perkins, Plastic Omnium (a French car part distributer), supermarket retailer Asda and Domino's Pizza are located at Omega.

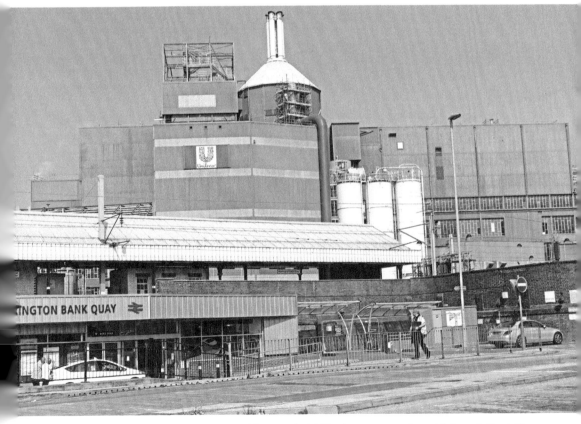

Few traditional industrial sites are visible in today's Warrington apart from Unilever's Bank Quay operation. It is still known locally as Crosfield's, despite being sold to their rivals in the 1920s.

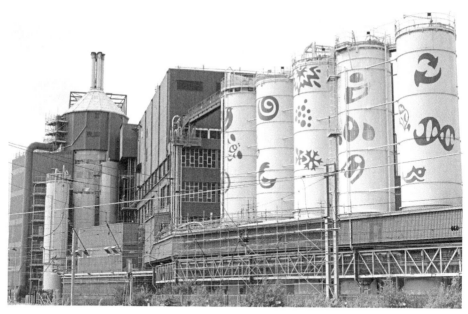

The sides of Unilever's five white towers have designs representing parts of their business. Production of Persil and Surf at Warrington is denoted by the long-sleeve shirt being laundered.

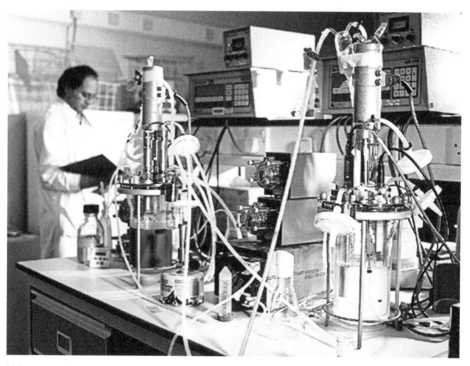

Warrington's reputation for world-leading scientific research continues with businesses including the nearby Daresbury research laboratory: accelerator science, bio-medicine, computing science and engineering.

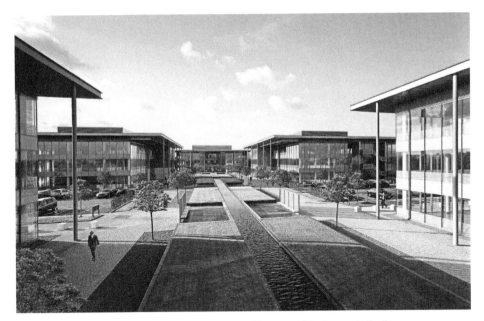

The offices at award-winning Bridgewater Place at Birchwood Park were purpose designed for the needs of modern business. From 2014–16 it was the site of the Hillsborough Inquest.

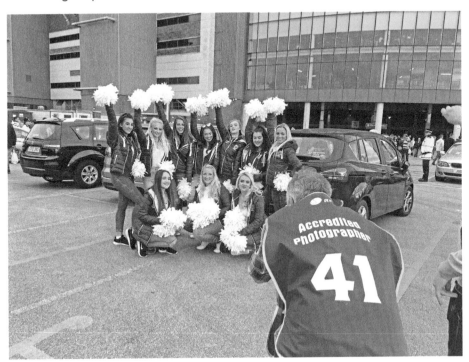

Deputy editor Gareth Dunning records and posts online photographer Dave Gillespie in action as part of *Warrington Guardian*'s live coverage of the 2016 Super League Grand Final at Old Trafford.

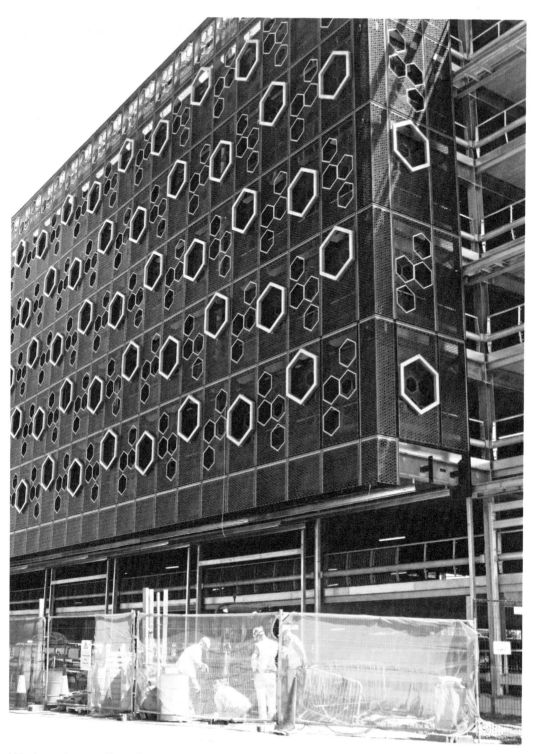

Work on the new Time Square development car park in June 2017 follows strict health and safety measures unknown to the workmen in Bridge Street a century earlier.

Also available from Amberley Publishing

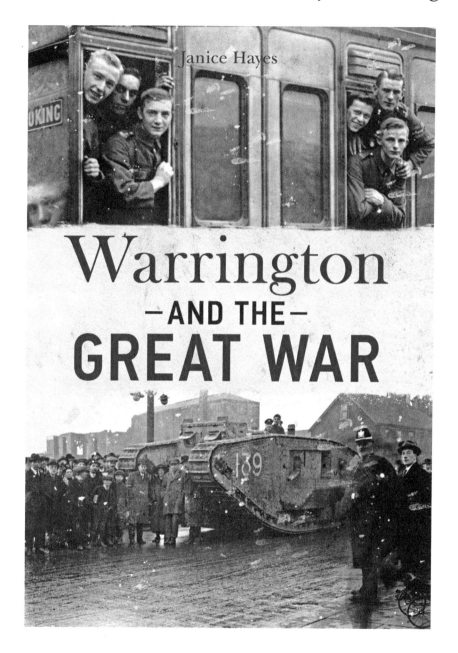

Janice Hayes

Warrington
-AND THE-
GREAT WAR

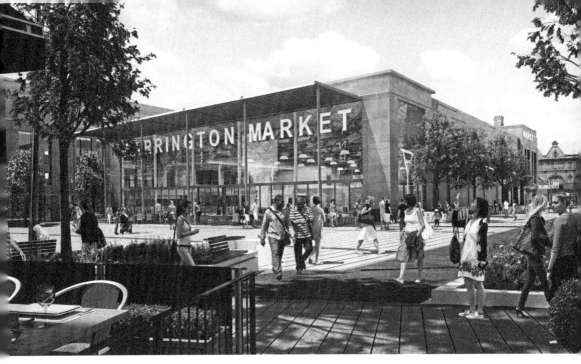

Twenty-first-century Warrington has ambitions to be a city. The Time Square development will create a new leisure and shopping destination while celebrating Warrington's heritage as a market town.

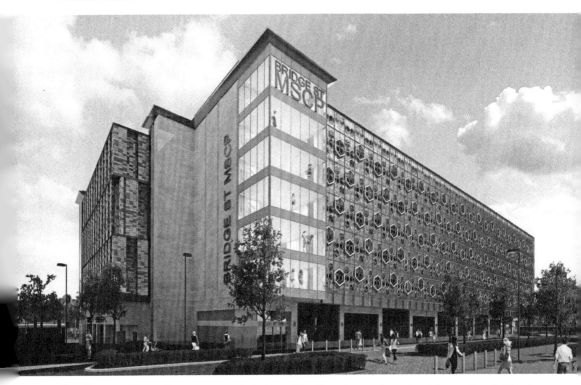

The façade of Time Square car park designed by Manchester-based architects Leach Rhodes Walker pays homage to Warrington's wire-making history while looking to the future of Warrington's new city centre.